SCOTNOTES
Number 11

The Poems of
Robert Henryson

by

Gerald Baird

Principal Teacher of English
Grove Academy, Broughty Ferry, Dundee

Association for Scottish Literary Studies 1996

Published by
Association for Scottish Literary Studies
c/o The Department of English
University of Aberdeen
Aberdeen AB9 2UB

First published 1996

A CIP catalogue for this title is available from the British Library

ISBN 0 948877 29 4

Subsidised by

THE SCOTTISH ARTS COUNCIL

Typeset by Roger Booth Associates, Hassocks, West Sussex
Printed by BPC AUP Aberdeen Ltd

CONTENTS

NOTE ON REFERENCES

Quotations and line references are based on *Robert Henryson: The Poems* edited by Denton Fox and published by the Clarendon Press Oxford in 1981 and 1987. An excellent paperback edition is available, containing the complete text of the poems, with a short introduction, simplified notes and a glossary.

EDITORS' FOREWORD

The *Scotnotes* booklets are a series of study guides to major Scottish writers and literary texts that are likely to be elements within literature courses. They are aimed at senior pupils in secondary schools and students in further education colleges and colleges of education. Consequently it is intended that, wherever possible, each booklet in the series will be written by a person who is not only an authority on the particular writer or text but also experienced in teaching at the relevant levels in schools or colleges. Furthermore, the editorial board, composed of members of the Schools and Further Education Committee of the Association for Scottish Literary Studies, considers the suitability of each booklet for the students in question. In preparing the series, the editors are conscious of the fact that for many years there has been a shortage of readily accessible critical notes for the general student of Scottish literature; and they intend that *Scotnotes* will grow as a series at the rate of about two booklets a year to meet this need and provide students with valuable aids to the understanding and appreciation of the key writers and major texts within the Scottish literary tradition.

Lorna Borrowman Smith
Elaine Petrie

INTRODUCTION

Robert Henryson is one of the most accomplished and enjoyable poets of the later Middle Ages, and a writer whose writings should be far better known than has been the case, particularly in his native Scotland, where he has been quite scandalously neglected. In recent years, however, there have been unmistakable signs that his work is beginning to gain the recognition it deserves: Denton Fox's edition of his works has provided a first-rate basis for the study of the texts, the inclusion of Henryson on the list of writers recommended for study for the Certificate of Sixth Year Studies has provided a vital stimulus for teaching Henryson in schools and the founding in Dunfermline of the Robert Henryson Society in 1993 not only is in itself a recognition of the growing interest in his work, but affords a focus for the steadily increasing activity connected with his name.

Henryson's reputation in Scotland should be as secure as Chaucer's is in England and it is hoped that these notes will assist and encourage many more people to study, and above all to enjoy, some of the finest poetry that has been written in Scotland or elsewhere.

BACKGROUND

What we know about Henryson

Our knowledge of the life of Robert Henryson is very limited indeed, particularly when contrasted with the information we have about his near-contemporaries, William Dunbar and Gavin Douglas. Dunbar's position in the household of James IV causes his name to appear in the records of the court, and many of his poems present us with his own view of his ambiguous position in society, while Douglas's membership of one of the great families of mediaeval Scotland and his own involvement in the murky politics of the period have made him one of the best-documented individuals of his day. Of Henryson, on the other hand, much is speculative and little is certain. One of the difficulties is that the name Robert Henryson (or Henderson) was a common name then as now, and it is seldom possible to identify our man unequivocally with any of the various Roberts who crop up in the fifteenth century. It is *possible* that the poet is the *Robertus Henrisone* recorded at the recently founded University of Glasgow in 1462; he is frequently referred to (by Dunbar, for example) as **Maister** *Robert Henrysoun,* which would indicate a university background. His association with Dunfermline seems as certain as anything about him; once again, Dunbar connects him with the Fife burgh, and in early editions of his poems he is called the schoolmaster of Dunfermline. This was a post of no little prestige and responsibility, to be master of the school connected with the great Benedictine abbey which, with St. Andrews Priory and Arbroath Abbey, was one of the richest foundations in mediaeval Scotland. The status attached to the post can also be seen in Henryson's role as a notary public in legal matters concerning the abbey. The poet then may be assumed to be a man of some importance in his area, closely involved in its public life. There is no certain information about his birth or death; about 1425 seems as good a guess as any for the former, and for the latter our best informant is once more Dunbar, who in about 1508 includes Henryson in his list of poets who have died.

How to read Henryson

(a) His language
Although reading the text of the poems can certainly present

problems for those unfamiliar with the language Henryson employs, too much has been made of the supposed difficulty of reading Middle Scots and not enough of the frequently surprising similarities to Scots as still spoken and pronounced in the twentieth century. The unfamiliarity arises very largely from the appearance of the words on the page, which may often seem strange (though no more so than Chaucer, for instance) but a feel for the *sound* of Modern Scots will often help to resolve any apparent difficulties. For example, knowing that the Modern Scots word for a paying guest is a *ludger* clarifies a phrase such as: *Quhen thay wer lugit thus ...* (F204).

The story of the Scots literary language is a fascinating study in itself, and there are several accounts of its nature and development which are well worth looking at, not only for their own sakes, but for the light they throw on the work of poets such as Henryson. A short list of some of these appears in the bibliography, but here it is sufficient to point out that a most useful short outline of the topic is to be found in the introduction to the readily-available *Concise Scots Dictionary*.

We must remember that in the end, the text only looks unfamiliar if it *is* unfamiliar: the more we read Henryson, or anyone else, the easier it becomes. As with any worthwhile study, familiarity will come with practice. In the meantime, there are several shortcuts to understanding which should be noted:

Three things to know about Henryson's Language

1 **Spelling variations** The number of actual words in Henryson which are unknown in either Modern Scots or Modern English is relatively small; far more common are words which have a modern equivalent partly concealed by the spelling or some other peculiarity of form, and being aware of these variations makes the text much more accessible. Remember that spelling was not generally standardised until the eighteenth century, and the same word may appear in various guises: the word we now spell *blood* may appear as *blude, blud* or *bluid*; the word *sweet*, as *sweit, sueit, suete* or *suet*, similarly, the simple word *if* will often appear in the guise of *gif, giff* or even *geue*, and so a certain degree of alertness is required of the reader.

2 **The Alphabet** Although the alphabet used by Henryson was much the same as ours, with a few minor differences, some

features should be noted: the letters *u*, and *v* (and occasionally *w*) are often interchangeable:

vse = use	vs = us	vntill = until
siluer = silver	euer = ever	haue = have

One understandable source of strangeness in the appearance of Henryson's text is the frequent presence of the letter ʒ (called *yogh*) which we no longer have in our alphabet. It usually represents the sound now represented by the consonant Y, in words such as ʒe or ʒour:

ʒe = ye   ʒour = your   ʒowth = youth   ʒeir = year

ʒe ar ʒour fatheris sone and air   F47
Fot all ʒour mowis, ʒe met anis with ʒour matche   F2555

3 **Equivalences** By far the most common cause of puzzlement occurs when a word takes a form slightly different from its modern equivalent, but when it is realised that many of these variations are regular in form, as is the case when learning a language like German, for instance, it becomes a matter of getting to know a few of these equivalences and most of the difficulties disappear:

i. The very common "quh" may look strange, but can be altered to modern "wh":

quhether = whether   quhair = where   quhat = what

Quhen we are sad quha sall vnto vs sing?   F503

ii. Many words ending in -*and* are present participles, and would today end with -*ing*:

scraipand = scraping
belangand = belonging
quaikand = quaking

... ane prettie fabill
Concludand with ane gude moralitie   F1386–7

iii. When a word ends in -*it*, this may well be a past participle or a past tense ending, equivalent to Modern English -*ed*: e.g.

callit = called   excludit = excluded   endit = ended

The volff chargit the scheip   F1245

One good example of this is to be found in *The Preaching of the Swallow* where Henryson gives a technical description of the preparation of flax:

> The lynt *ryipit*, the carll *pullit* the lyne,
> *Rippillit* the bollis, and in beitis set,
> It *steipit* in the burne, and *dryit* syne,
> And with ane bittill *knokkit* it and bet,
> Syne *swingillit* it weill, and *hekkillit* in the flet;
> His wyfe it span, and *twynit* it in to threid,
> Off quhilk the fowlar nettis maid in deid.   F1825–31

iv. The suffix *-is* is equivalent to modern *-s*, either as a plural or a verb ending:

> I sall off it mak mittenis to my lufis
> Till hald my handis hait quhair euer I be   F2072–3

> The hennis are warkis that fra ferme faith proceidis   F2437

v. Many words have equivalences of sound, rather than of spelling; that is to say, the sound in Middle Scots is consistently rendered by an equivalent sound in Modern Scots or English. Three examples will make the point, and cover many of the occurrences:

Firstly, the sound represented by the spelling *dd* in Scots is often equivalent to English *th*:

> wedder = weather   widderit = withered   gadderit = gathered

> The wedder is warme and fair   (R&M 98)
> ... now widderit and ago   (T238)
> Thus quhen thay gadderit war   (T264)

Similarly, the Scots word *kirk*, equivalent to the English *church* (and the German *Kirche*) illustrates the frequent use of the sound represented by *k* where English would use *ch*:

> busk = bush   kist = chest   sic = such

> ... vnder busk and breir   (F166)
> Amang the cheis and meill, in ark and kist   (F175)
> I ʒow beseik   (F689)

Thirdly, the vowel sound represented by *ai* in Scots, sometimes by *a*, is often equivalent to the sound represented by *oa* or *oe* in English:

straikand / stroking:

> Straikand his wame aganis the sonis heit   F759

gait / goat:

> Quhen this wes said, the keipar of the gait   F761

da, ra / doe, roe (deer):

> The da, the ra, the hornit hart, the hynd   F900

aitis / oats:

> Off ryip aitis, off barlie, peis and quheit?   F2792

wa / woe:

> Gif scho in hart was wa aneuch ...   T350

Mention should also be made here of the matter of pronunciation of the indefinite article *ane*, which performs the functions of the two words *a* and *an* in English (as well as the word *one*) and should be pronounced in the same way, that is, like the English word *a* before a consonant, and the English word *an* before a vowel. The first line of the *Testament* is a good example of the *a* pronunciation:

> Ane doolie sessoun to ane cairfull dyte

whereas line 61 has the *an* version:

> To brek my sleip ane vther quair I tuik

If such lines are read aloud as they should be, it will be seen that their supposed strangeness disappears entirely, being a matter of spelling only.

Familiarity with these few examples will help to clarify many of the surface difficulties which new readers of Henryson may experience.

Six key words to learn

1. *gar* (*garris/gart/gert* ...) (+ infinitive) to cause to do something

> To blyth the spreit and gar the tyme be schort   F21
> Schouris of haill gart fra the north discend   T6

2. *Can/couth/culd/coud* (+ infinitive) is equivalent to a past tense; one might substitute the word *did*, for a modern version of the past tense:

> Orpheus in coud ga   (Orpheus in did go)   O&E 309
> ane swallow loud couth cry   F1734
> the wickit wind can blaw   F1832
>
> On nicht thay ran and on the day can sleip,
> Quhill in the morning, or the lauerock sang,
> Thay fand the town, and in blythlie couth gang   F257–9

3 *quhill/quhyle* ... is of course equivalent to modern *while*, but there are three distinct meanings in Middle Scots:

   i   while:

      Pray we thairfoir quhill we ar in this lyfe   F1944

   ii   until:

      This maid thay merie, quhill thay micht na mair   F288

   iii   now ... then/one minute ... the next ... :

      Quhyle to, quhyle fra, quhyle doukit up agane   F2892

Remember Burns's *Tam o'Shanter*:

      Whiles holding fast his guid blue bonnet,
      Whiles crooning o'er some auld Scots sonnet,
      Whiles glow'ring round wi' prudent cares,
      Lest bogles catch him unawares.

See *The Two Mice*, where two of these forms appear within a couple of lines:

      For quhylis thay leuch, and quhylis for ioy thay gret,
      Quhyle kissit sweit, quhylis in armis plet,
      And thus thay fure quhill soberit wes their mude   F193–195

4. *or/are/ere/air*: adverb: *previously*

      This Tantalus, of quhom I spak of are   O&E 519
      The samin birdis as I haif said ȝow air   F1784

5. *reid/rede*: as well as the modern *read* or *red*, this word can also mean to advise, or advice:

      Remoue, I reid, or ellis ȝe will be slane   F1857
      On thame that will not tak counsall nor reid   F1883

6. *swa*: a very common word, simply representing the modern *so*:

      'Giff it be swa, ȝe ar at eis,' quod scho.   F280
      Swa wes his father, and his grandschir als.   F809

Six more words to know!

As has been indicated above, there is a limited number of actual new words to be learned when reading Henryson, rather than forms of words already known, but one area where difficulties can arise is in those words which look familiar, but whose meaning has changed considerably in the intervening five hundred years, words which the French call *faux amis*, or false friends.

Here is a sample of six words which look reassuringly familiar, but which Henryson often uses in a sense rather different from the modern usage:

i. sentence: this important word can mean *meaning*:

> Bot of the inward sentence and intent
> Of this fabill ...   F117–8

or *piece of writing*:

> Ɣyt men may find ane gude moralitee
> In this sentence, thocht it ane fabill be.   F2425–6

ii. sillie/sely/selie: an earlier version of the modern word *silly*, but meaning something like *pitiable, helpless, powerless or innocent*:

> This selie scheip may present the figure
> Of pure commounis ...   F1258–9
> The selie lamb was meik and innocent   F2625

iii. curage/curageous: as well as the modern meaning, there are usually overtones of *desire, lust, sexual longing*:

> And in the auld the curage doif and deid   T32
> And in that craft hardy and curageouse   O&E492

iv. cair/cairfull: This word is much stronger than our modern sense of being concerned or of taking care, and is closer to *distress, sorrow, misery*:

> Ane doolie sessoun to a cairfull dyte
> Suld correspond and be equivalent   T1–2
> Thair cairfull sang and lamentatioun.   F1877

v. sad: Another word which was much stronger in the past: *serious, sorrowful:*

> With sad materis sum merines to ming
> Accordis weill ...   F26–7
>
> Richt so vnder ane fabill figurall
> Sad sentence men may seik ...
> F1099–1100

vi. but: A very common sense of this word is *without*:

> And that is euidence aneuch, but dout.   F1086
> And to ane wod I went allone but gyde   F1327

Acquiring familiarity with the language of any poet who wrote five hundred years ago will necessarily take some application on the part of the student, but the task can be made considerably less onerous if the nature of the difficulties is clearly understood. The information above will help to focus attention on areas which will repay a comparatively small investment of time and energy.

(b) How to get started: The Two Mice

For those who have read no Henryson before, it might be helpful to begin with a single poem and work methodically through a set of questions designed to bring out some of the ideas and techniques which are to be found in his work. This example is based on *The Two Mice*.

This fable is fairly simple in structure, involving only two speaking characters, a straightforward narrative, and a short *Moralitas*.

1. What differences in the lives of the two sisters are made clear in the first two stanzas? Answer in your own words.

The Country Mouse	The Town Mouse
....	....
....	....
....	....

2. Identify THREE techniques by which Henryson makes the Town Mouse's journey in the fourth stanza seem long and hard. (Do not simply quote; state what Henryson *does*):

i ....

ii ....

iii ....

3. Quote three separate adjectives which indicate the poor nature of the Country Mouse's dwelling:

i .... ii .... iii ....

4. When the Country Mouse produces her *nuttis and peis, in
steid of spyce*, how does the narrator guide the reader's reaction
before the Town Mouse speaks?

....

5. The disagreement between the sisters over the food is the
occasion for some delectable social comedy. Pick out some phrases
which show the tension which has arisen between them:

....

6. With what argument in lines 225–238 does the rural mouse
try to win her sister round to the food on offer? (In your own
words).

....

7. Pick out two examples of sarcasm in the Town Mouse's final
speech before they leave:

i .... ii ....

8. When they get to the town, and see the abundance all around,
what reservation does the Country Mouse have about the way her
sister lives?

....

9. In what way are lines 290–1 different from the surrounding
lines?

....

10. What saved them when the spenser came in?

....

11. What evidence is there that the Town Mouse is accustomed to
living in danger?

....

12. By what means does Henryson emphasise what *Gib Hunter,
our iolie cat* did to the Country Mouse?

....

13. How did she escape? ....

14. The Country Mouse repeats the same idea in different words
three times in lines 344–6; what is this idea?

....

15. Quote the two phrases by which Henryson re-introduces the
narrator towards the end of the fable:

....

....

16. How does Henryson establish a relationship between the
narrator and the reader in the moralitas?

....

17. What does Henryson say about human happiness in the first
stanza of the moralitas?

....

18. For what reason does he appear to quote Solomon in the last
stanza?

....

19. What is similar about the last line of each of these stanzas,
and for what purpose?

....

20. So, in a sentence, what is the moral of this story?

....

The Middle Ages

The phrase **Middle Ages** is usually taken to refer to the centuries
from the end of the so-called Dark Ages (the period of the long
decline of the Roman Empire and of the great invasions of Western
Europe by the eastern and northern peoples like the Vikings,
Vandals, Goths) and the beginnings of the modern world, i.e. from
about 900 AD till about 1500. Henryson therefore was writing in
the last decades of the mediaeval period, just before the excitingly
invigorating new forms of learning emanating principally from
southern Europe, to which we conventionally give the label the
Renaissance, began to have their effect in Scotland.

The Middle Ages were fascinating centuries, full of interest
and life, yet it is not easy for us now to see the world in the
manner which was normal for all people in Europe during the
Middle Ages, and which shaped so many of the ideas and
attitudes which are found in the writings of Robert Henryson.
This is because Henryson lived on the other side of the great
divides in human affairs which had already begun to take place
towards the end of the Middle Ages and which taken together
mark off the mediaeval period from the modern.

To gain some insight into the kind of Europe inhabited by
Henryson and other mediaeval writers it is necessary to imagine
a world in many ways with more defined limits, with more
universally shared beliefs and assumptions, more certain of itself
and its purpose, and seemingly less chaotic and aimless than our
own. Various social forces and movements intervened to separate
us from the certainties of that age and to make it difficult for us
even to recognise many of its most basic ways of perceiving the
world and the place of human beings in it. Having an awareness
of some at least of these factors will make Henryson's world
considerably more accessible.

The spread of information, which might be taken as the lifeblood
of the twentieth century, was effected in much the same manner
throughout the Middle Ages as it had been in classical times. Any
writings thought worthy of preservation or transmission were
copied laboriously by hand, at great expense of time, effort and
money, and with all the inevitable errors in transcription which
human copying entails, the consequences of these being found in
early versions of Henryson's work. The development (in Europe)
of **Printing** began in Germany in about 1465, during Henryson's
lifetime, and was recognised immediately by the established

powers of church and state as a very dangerous development, which had to be controlled. In Scotland, printing was banned until James IV gave limited permission in 1507. For the first time thousands of copies of any text, pious or subversive, could be produced very quickly, and furthermore could be produced at a relatively low cost, making ideas, for good or ill, available to a vastly greater number without the intervention of an authorised interpreter, such as a clergyman.

Henryson was living in a Scotland which was as yet not significantly affected by the **Renaissance** (literally, *re-birth*) in art and literature. This was a phenomenon which began in Italy, and spread rapidly across the continent. The rediscovery and systematic study of the classic works of the Greeks and Romans in literature, sculpture and architecture among other arts and sciences, and the development of humanistic techniques of analysis and interpretation provided an unprecedented stimulus to new ways of thinking in the West, and indirectly produced a challenge to the authority of church and state alike by demonstrating that goodness, beauty and wisdom were by no means the preserve of nominally Christian societies, which indeed were often put to shame by the examples of fortitude, selflessness and piety in the persons of pagan writers and philosophers. These tensions were to play no small part in the religious controversies of the coming years.

The centrality of Europe and European culture in the experience of the world was assumed in an age which had little sense of the actual extent of the planet. The **Voyages of Discovery**, that is to say, the various ocean journeys, often undertaken by Portuguese navigators, radically enlarged current ideas of the size of the world, and the relative importance of Europe within it. Columbus's voyage to the Americas in 1492 had a profound effect when it was realised that there was another, totally unknown world in existence, one which had its distinctive flora and fauna, as well as its indigenous systems for the regulation of human life, which were not likely to be acceptable to a Europe already grievously divided over the enforcement of "correct" systems of behaviour and morals.

Such changes in the way the world is perceived had already begun to take place in Henryson's lifetime; after his death, changes just as momentous continued, compounding the differences between his age and ours, and thereby making our task all the more complex.

For example, it is apparent from many references in his works (e.g. *Testament* 147, *O&E* 219ff) that Henryson employed the mediaeval model of the physical universe. It is true that many of the astronomical references in the poems are merely examples of conventional poetic imagery rather than a statement of actual belief, such as the passage on the horses of the sun, *Testament* 204–217. On the other hand he also frequently uses the normal vocabulary and concepts of mediaeval cosmology. The two kinds of writing may be seen together in the introduction to *The Preaching of the Swallow:*

> The firmament payntit with sternis cleir
> From eist to west rolland in cirkill round,
> And euerilk planet in his proper spheir,
> In mouing makand harmonie and sound   F1657–1660

– where the word *payntit* is no more than a conventional metaphor, while the spheres and their music are standard features of the generally accepted structure of the universe in Henryson's day.

Furthermore, Henryson's writings frequently portray a partly astrological, rather than a solely astronomical, vision of planetary motion; that is to say, the movements of the planetary bodies were thought to have an influence on events on earth. The fox in *The Fox and the Wolf*, for example, is able to assess:

> Quhat influence and constellatioun
> Wes lyke to fall the eirth adoun   F645–6

while the actual physical intervention of the planets in *The Testament of Cresseid* is accompanied by the statement that they:

> ... hes power of all thing generabill,
> To reull and steir be thair greit influence
> Wedder and wind, and coursis variabill.   T148–150

The mediaeval theory of planetary motion posited nine gigantic hollow and transparent spheres which revolved around the earth at their centre. Each sphere had one of the seven planets attached to it, in order of their increasing distance from earth: Moon, Mercury, Venus, Sun, Mars, Jupiter, Saturn. The eighth sphere held the stars, and the ninth, which controlled the motion of all the others, was known as the *Primum Mobile*. In their motion these spheres created celestial music, beyond the hearing of human ears; as they look up at the night sky, Lorenzo tells Jessica in Shakespeare's *The Merchant of Venice*:

> There's not the smallest orb which thou behold'st
> But in his motion like an angel sings.   (V,i)

A knowledge of this system is taken for granted both in the visitation of the gods to Cresseid and in Orpheus's journey to the heavens.

Not long after Henryson's death the Polish astronomer **Copernicus** asserted that the observed orbits of the planets could only be made to make sense if the earth and the other planets went round the sun, and not the sun round the earth. Gradually the belief spread that the earth was not after all the centre of the universe, and that therefore the earlier view of an intimate little system where all the observable universe centred on the earth and indeed whose very purpose was to provide the earth with a physical and moral context, with God above, like a stern father, constantly watching everything that went on in the human world, became psychologically untenable when it was realised that there was nothing special in physical or astronomical terms about the earth. The work of **Galileo** and **Kepler** confirmed his findings, and with the invention of the telescope (about 1600) anyone who wished could witness phenomena which throughout the Middle Ages had been regarded as heretical ideas, since they denied the perfection of all celestial bodies: the mountains on the moon, sunspots, the elliptical (and thence imperfect) rather than the perfectly circular orbits of the planets, the moons of Jupiter. (When Galileo watched the little moons circle the planet, the Jovian sphere, and hence the planetary spheres generally, vanished with his observations.) Hence the old gods and the old imagery began to give way to the new: the image of Saturn in the common mind today is of its rings, rather than of:

> The ice schoklis that fra his hair doun hang
> Was wonder greit, and as ane speir als lang.   T160–1

This is by no means to say that Henryson was an astrologer as it might be understood today. Indeed, in *Orpheus and Eurydice* he vigorously attacks

> wichcraft, spaying, and sorsery,
> And superstitioun of astrolegy   O&E588–9

contrasting it with *trew astronomy*, but that he then defines as

> Be moving of the speiris in the sky   O&E597

which understandably implies a pre-Copernican universe.

Henryson, like most mediaeval writers, was fully aware of the
various abuses in the church of his day, and is critical of them.
When Orpheus visits hell, for instance:

> There fand he mony pape and cardinall
> In haly kirk quhilk dois abusion;
> And archbischopis in thair pontificall
> Be symony and wrang intrusion;
> Abbotis and men of all religion,
> For euill disponyng of thair placis rent,
> In flambe of fyre were bitterly turment.   (O&E 338–344)

but the criticism is limited to the abuses, not to the very nature of
the institution of the church itself, which was to be the reason for
the conflict, the *cause de guerre,* in the centuries following. The
Reformation (which could not have taken place as it did without
the invention of printing) radically altered the minds of mankind
with regard to their ideas about God and the church. The Bible
was made readily available in Protestant countries for individuals
to read for themselves, which had the effect of greatly weakening
the power of the church. Few countries experienced a reformation
as thorough or as far-reaching in its effects as in Scotland; just as
many of our older churches to this day bear the physical scars in
the form of empty niches where statues once stood, similarly
many of our pre-reformation literary artefacts were destroyed,
suppressed or radically altered (as happened with a number of
Henryson's poems) to remove any taint of Romanism.

A notable feature of Henryson's poetry, by no means unusual
in his day, is his frequent appeal to learned authority, such as the
explicit references throughout the Fables not only to Aesop of
course, but also to Solomon (F391), to Aristotle (F1636), to the
Bible generally and to various unspecified sources, like the
putative quair in which he purports to have read an account of the
end of Cresseid (T61). Over the centuries **modern scientific
method** (the procedure by which a hypothesis is formed and then
tested against the observable facts) began to take the place of
superstition, alchemy and the appeal to learned authorities (such
as Aristotle) as a means of providing an authoritative explanation
of natural phenomena. Modern chemistry developed out of
mediaeval alchemy, and its system of elements replaced

> The fyre, the air, the watter, and the ground   F1661

as the basis for the study of matter, and thence, of human biology
and psychology. These modern scientific disciplines eventually
superseded such pseudo-sciences as the *phisnomy* in which the

little mouse put his trust (F2824), or the Theory of Humours, referred to when Saturn lays his wand on Cresseid, changing:

Thy moisture and thy heit in cald and dry.   T318

According to mediaeval physiology, one's temperament was determined by the proportion of the four humours: sanguine, phlegmatic, choleric or melancholy, represented respectively by the predominance in the body of blood, phlegm, choler and black bile. These humours in turn were composed of two of the basic elements: hot, cold, dry, wet, which were the physical basis of all living creatures, and the humours altered under the influence of planetary combinations.

As the scientific method proved its worth, other areas of application arose: the work of Isaac Newton in England established Physics in the same way as Hutton's work in Scotland introduced the study of Geology; for the first time, in the eighteenth century, some people at least began to suggest that the world might be more than merely five or six thousand years old! Remember Burns's Holy Willie asking his God:

What was I, or my generation,
That I should get sic exaltation?
I, wha deserv'd most just damnation
          For broken laws
Sax thousand years ere my creation,
          Thro' Adam's cause!

There is a temptation to regard rural life before industrialisation as a bucolic idyll, and our popular culture often presents country life as simpler and happier than urban life. This tension between the two is of course the basis of *The Two Mice*, and earlier examples can be found at least as far back as Roman times. What is more difficult for us to realise is the extent to which the townsman of earlier days was perforce a countryman as well; not only does Henryson demonstrate an intimate familiarity with the behaviour of animals domestic and wild, however stylised; the master of the abbey school of Dunfermline is also able to demonstrate his detailed knowledge of the processes involved in the production of flax (F1825–1830), Dunfermline being the main centre in Scotland of that industry. Even so late a writer as Thomas Hardy could make a point (in Chapter 14 of *The Mayor of Casterbridge*) of how intimately his Casterbridge, "a place deposited in the block upon a corn-field", coexisted with its agricultural hinterland. The **Industrial Revolution** which began in Britain in the eighteenth century had affected much of

Europe by the nineteenth, and from this period come the great
movements of population away from the land and into the cities,
with all the associated problems of overcrowding, poverty,
malnutrition, pollution and crime with which we still grapple.

Possibly the mediaeval concept we might find hardest to adapt
to was the belief that everything was really going to continue
much as it always had done. Nowadays we are accustomed to
change; change has become the norm of our lives; we expect there
constantly to be new inventions, new social patterns, new
countries emerging, new alliances, new forms of medicine,
discoveries in space research and so on, and in our personal lives
we are not surprised if we change our jobs several times in a
lifetime, move from one country to another, even marry more than
once. The mediaeval expectation was quite different. Each
individual had an unchanging place in the unchanging scheme of
things:

God	The Supreme Being
Angels	Pure spirits
Human Beings	Part spirit, part animal, with the powers of growth, movement and rational thought
Animals	With the power of growth and movement
Plants	With the power of growth
Inanimate Objects	Mere existence

The intermediate position of human beings in this system
accounted both for the marvellous qualities that human beings
could show (courage, charity, self-sacrifice, foresight, creativity,
piety and so on) and for the baser elements of human nature
(greed, lust, avarice, envy ...). The spiritual life of any individual
was a matter of trying to overcome the animal nature and
aspiring to the spiritual state, a conflict which is expressed
particularly aptly in the Fables.

It was convenient for the establishment that this hierarchical
system mirrored the feudal social system of the times, wherein
each individual had a pre-determined place from which it was
very difficult to move:

God
The King
The Nobility
The Gentry
Merchants/Burghers
Tradesmen
Peasants

Much of the humour of *The Two Mice*, for instance arises from the tension between them. One has apparently gone up in the world, but at the cost of ever-present danger. This mouse:

Was gild brother and made a fre burges   F172

while her sister claims:

I keip the ryte and custome of my dame.   F215

It is surely significant that Henryson's moralitas condemns:

thay quhilk clymmis vp maist hie,
And not content with small possessioun.   F371–2

Parallel to the social structure was the structure of **the mediaeval church**, one of the most complex organisations of the period. The church had an influence which pervaded every aspect of life in a way that has not been possible for the last four hundred years. Before printing and the Reformation made the Bible available to anyone who wished to read it, scripture was interpreted for the people by the clergy, which gave them a greater power even than that of life and death: the power of controlling one's destination in the afterlife. The mediaeval church was a gigantic affair, ranging from intellectual and theological geniuses like St. Thomas Aquinas and genuinely saintly visionaries like St. Francis of Assisi, and all kinds of loyal, trustworthy and hardworking priests, monks and nuns on the one hand, and on the other, as in any human institution, corrupt individuals interested only in their own financial or social success. Every citizen would have dealings on almost a daily basis with members of the clergy, who were often the only literate members of the community, a factor which gave them even greater power, since they controlled education as well. The power of the church both in social and spiritual matters is assumed throughout Henryson's work, especially the Fables, from the swallow who represents *The halie preichour*, to Freir Volff Waitskaith, to the *selie lamb* who unavailingly quotes scripture in an attempt to save his life, to the casual slight on the friars in the concluding moralitas.

What, then, was life like for people in Scotland in the time of Henryson? It was in many ways very similar to that elsewhere in Europe, Scotland being at that time an independent nation, sharing in all the great movements of the time, belonging to the universal (Roman Catholic) church, trading with the Netherlands and the Baltic states in particular, and European ways of living and thinking were normal. The running sore of uneasy relationships with England, frequently breaking into open conflict, remained unresolved throughout the period. The fifteenth century was, however, a time of great change in Scotland. The first three Scottish universities were founded at this time, a development which was to have profound effects in the future. In the political world, since the return of James I in 1424 from his lengthy captivity in England, the monarchs had been attempting, with some success, to strengthen the power of the throne while reducing the threat from the gangsterism of over-mighty nobles. It has been suggested, and disputed, that a number of Henryson's poems (*The Lion and the Mouse*, for instance) contain references to events of his own time, and particularly to struggles between king and nobles in the reign of James III (1460–1488). In spite of the demoralising succession of minorities the kingship which James IV inherited on his accession in 1488 was more securely based than before, and he had the opportunity to involve himself and his court in some of the new-fangled ideas emanating from Renaissance Italy, before the cataclysmic disaster of Flodden in 1513 brought the century to a belated end and ushered in the new uncertainties of the sixteenth century.

Some Literary Background

Henryson has been called a "bookish" writer, in that his major works are all based on the works of other writers, and contain many references to writers and writings. To some authors he pays specific tribute: Chaucer, Aesop/Gualterus, Aristotle, Boethius, Trivet, and others. In addition, the unattributed influence of many writers has been suggested in his poems, including that of Plato, Macrobius, Lydgate and possibly Caxton. A third area of influence is the knowledge he so evidently displays of, for example, the Bible, classical mythology and the legal system.

The literary culture within which he operated was, as his works illustrate, both sophisticated and versatile. Two main strands in the structure of Henryson's poetry should be acknowledged. The first poetry written in the Germanic tongues in these islands depended on alliteration for its formal control, and the Anglian form of Old English from which Scots eventually developed shared this fundamental structural device. After the Norman Conquest new French modes began to be introduced, first to England, then further north, in which the organisation of poetry was based, not on alliteration, but on the counting of syllables and the use of rhyme. As might be expected, the two traditions frequently fused, so that the first little fragment of poetry that exists in Scots employs both alliteration and also syllabic symmetry and rhyme. The first major flowering of writing in Scots was John Barbour's poem *The Brus* on the life and achievements of King Robert I, a *tour de force* in no fewer than twenty books of vigorous octosyllabic couplets. Barbour, a contemporary of Geoffrey Chaucer in England, lived from about 1320 to 1395, and demonstrated that the language was a responsive medium capable of carrying the considerable demands he laid upon it. A yet more complex predecessor of Henryson's work was *The Kingis Quair*, ostensibly written by James I, and demonstrating mastery of *rime-royal*, or Rhyme Royal, an elegant seven-line stanza with the rhyme scheme *ababbcc*, used by Chaucer in his *Troilus and Criseyde*. *The Kingis Quair* contains many fashionable features of the period which Henryson was also to employ, such as the dream vision, the inspiration from reading a book, the *locus amoenus*, or pleasant garden setting, the opening in early summer, the formal list of animals and the intervention of classical deities.

Much of Henryson's work is in Rhyme Royal (the Fables and the Testament, all but a few stanzas) but he also very frequently uses alliteration, giving himself the more difficult task of having to consider both the beginnings and the ends of words:

> The ground wes grene, and as the gold it glemis,
> With gresis growand gudelie, grit, and gay,
> The spyce thay spred to spring on euerilk spray.   F868–70

Nature poetry, and especially descriptions of winter, seemed to call for alliteration in verse:

> The wynter come, the wickit wind can blaw,
> The woddis grene wer wallowit with the weit,
> Baith firth and fell with froistys wer maid faw,
> Slonkis and slaik maid slidderie with the sleit;
> The foulis fair, for falt thay fell off feit—

> On bewis bair it wes na bute to byde,
> Bot hyit vnto housis thame to hyde.   F1832–8

The narrative part of *Orpheus and Eurydice* is written in Rhyme Royal, while the moralitas is in ten-syllable rhyming couplets, the form chosen by Chaucer for much of *The Canterbury Tales*, while in *Robene and Makyne* and *The Garmont of Gud Ladeis* Henryson employs a form of the Ballad Metre. The fashion for revival of the old alliterative mode is also represented in his work, by *Sum Practysis of Medecyne*, written in the old thirteen-line alliterative stanza.

The technical excellence of Henryson's poetry is one of the most important factors contributing to its reputation, and any student of his work should be aware of the skill involved in employing the various formats which he uses.

THE FABLES

Henryson's thirteen fables form part (some would say the literary culmination) of an ancient oral and literary tradition of using animals to represent human behaviour in stories. The continuing popularity of this device is attested today by the use of animals in nursery rhymes, children's stories and cartoons, and the reason is clear to see: the advantage lies in the simplification of complex human affairs to the identification of the animal characters with easily recognisable traits (the fox is cunning, the wolf rapacious, Garfield is slothful and greedy &c) which allows children to learn about human conduct without having to deal with the mystifying and often contradictory complexities of adult behaviour. It also has the advantage in adult writing of permitting the author to concentrate on single aspects of character uncomplicated by the need for artistic verisimilitude. Orwell's *Animal Farm*, for instance, is an excellent modern example of a text intended for adults, deceptively simple yet dealing with complex aspects of human behaviour such as the exploitation of the innocent and the misuse of power, but expressed through simple characters like Boxer, the loyal and hard-working carthorse, and the tyrannical Napoleon.

A measure of the complex and ambitious nature of Henryson's work is afforded by a glance at the two best known fabulists, or writers of fables, in the European tradition: Aesop's fables (in the form in which Henryson read them) generally run to perhaps a dozen lines or so of Latin; those of the great seventeenth-century French writer La Fontaine to a bit more, maybe thirty or forty lines on average. Most children come across some of Aesop's fables in one form or another, and most French people are able to recite some of La Fontaine's fables which they have learned at school. It is no deficiency in Henryson which causes his vastly more ambitious enterprise to be the least known of the three.

The 2975 lines of the Fables constitute a large body of work, one which might well be seen as daunting, so it may help to have some awareness of the overall shape of the work: an introduction (the Prologue) in which Henryson explains what he's about, then the thirteen fables, each followed by a moralitas (sometimes running to as much as sixty or seventy lines) in which the point of the fable is interpreted for the reader, not always quite as we might expect.

The Sources of the Fables

Although Henryson would have heard animal stories in many forms, it seems likely that his work is based on *two* main sources: his debt to the fables of Aesop is evident from the homage he explicitly pays in a number of places, but he also took many ideas, events and characters from the wilder, more violent stories which accumulated around foxes and wolves in the early Middle Ages, many assembled under the heading of the *Roman de Renard.*

It has been suggested that Henryson began by intending a translation of some at least of the tales of Aesop he had come across, then later added the Reynardian material; however it came about, there is no doubt that the two traditions are strongly represented.

Aesop is a shadowy, perhaps a legendary, figure and perhaps no more than a device to group together popular folk stories already two thousand years old in Henryson's time and which shared many common elements. The putative real person called Aesop is said to have lived in Phrygia in the sixth century BC, which may be no more than an indication of the antiquity of the tales he is credited with. Many of these would have been orally transmitted, but at various periods collections were made, particularly in the Roman period and in the early Middle Ages. There is little doubt that the version with which Henryson would have been familiar was the Latin collection made by one Gualterus Anglicus (Walter the Englishman) (line 28 of the Prologue is taken directly from that version). It is also probable that Henryson thought of Aesop as a Latin poet, from the words he gives Aesop himself to speak in *The Lion and the Mouse*:

> 'My sone,' said he, 'I am of gentill blude;
> My natall land is Rome, withoutin nay ... '   1370–1

The overall feel of the fables with a Reynardian source is quite distinctive: the cunning fox uses his wits to get the better of the brutal wolf or the gullible human, and we are in a world of charming rogues, violent deeds, farcical incidents and eventual come-uppance for the offender.

Whatever caused Henryson to take his inspiration from these two sources, it seems to be the case that he consciously patterned the overall shape of the Fables. It has often been pointed out that the order of the Fables seems to be symmetrical:

Fable number: 1 2 3 4 5 6 7 8 9 10 11 12 13
Source: Aesop I Renard I Aesop I Renard I Aesop

Furthermore, the central fable numerically (*The Lion and the Mouse*) is marked off as bearing special significance in other ways: it has a lengthy preamble in which the narrator has a dream, involving a personal appearance by Aesop himself in which Aesop is invited not only to tell the tale, but to supply the moralitas.

Intriguingly, there are two hundred stanzas before and two hundred stanzas after this tale, so the chances of coincidence are not high. This arrangement could of course be the work not of the poet, but of a later editor, but it is clear that some at least of the tales are in Henryson's intended order: the end of the Prologue leads explicitly into the tale of *The Cock and the Jasp*; the first stanza of the fourth fable (*The Fox and the Wolf*) refers back to the events of the previous fable, as does the first stanza of the fifth. The final fable in this order is plainly intended to be the final one.

It is likely, therefore, that the Fables as we now have them form a carefully organised whole, bearing in mind their grouping in order of their sources, their numerological symmetry, and the few explicit remarks that Henryson has left in the text. Whether this has merely a decorative function or some deeper purpose is a matter for conjecture.

The Prologue

These nine introductory stanzas are Henryson's statement of intent and as such merit close study. They raise a number of crucial issues which are dealt with in detail throughout the work. He begins by confronting immediately, as if to ward off expected criticism, the central problem of art since at least the time of Plato: how can what is not true have merit? The concessive clause of the first words goes straight to the heart of the matter:

> Thocht fein3eit fabils of ald poetre
> Be not al grunded vpon truth ...   1–2

but the two lines conceding the validity of the objections to poetry are more than counterbalanced by the remaining five, which make three main points:

i   the aesthetic attraction of art – the *polite termes* (i.e. the polished language) which are *Richt plesand* ii the moral justification: the purpose of *feinʒeit fabils* was to reprove human beings for their *misleuing* (their living in the wrong way)

iii the means by which they did this was *be figure of ane vther thing* (i.e. metaphorically or symbolically)

It is a measure of the importance which Henryson and other mediaeval writers gave to the necessity of establishing their moral credentials that the following three stanzas are given over to emphasising this central concern, each containing a metaphorical expression of the idea, and a restatement of the basic idea, introduced on each occasion by the link word *sa*: Just as flowers and corn will break through tough ground, so a fruitful meaning will emerge from *the subtell dyte of poetry*; just as a hard nutshell contains the toothsome kernel, so *ane feinʒeit fabill* may contain *ane doctrine wyse aneuch*; just as a bow which is always bent loses its flexibility, so does a mind which is always concerned with solemn matters. Having established the seriousness of his purpose, he now turns to Aesop, clinching his argument by quoting a line (1.28) from Gualterus (or from Aesop, as he would believe) which states: *Serious matters appear more sweetly smiling with humour.*

The following two stanzas (ll.29–42) deal with the poet's own position in this work. He sets up a deferential relationship towards his readers: *my maisteris, with ʒour leif/Submitting me to ʒour correctioun*, and announces his projected translation. The mention of a *lord* who supposedly requested him to undertake the translation may be seen as a conventional expression of modesty, that he would not have contemplated taking on such a task without aristocratic sanction. This modesty *topos*, a device also known as *excusatio*, is continued when this highly sophisticated poet protests that he must write *In hamelie language and in termes rude*, because he never understood *eloquence /Nor rethorike*, and indeed he invites the reader to amend anything which he has left imperfect.

Stanzas seven and eight (ll.43–56) come to the central theme of the Fables:

> How mony men in operatioun
> Ar like to beistis in conditioun.   48–9

– that is to say, that human beings in their behaviour are like beasts in character. With this we enter the battleground of the fables: human beings have the capacity and the free will to behave like angels, and demonstrate many angelic qualities like courage, selflessness, generosity and so forth, but are constantly dragged back to the merely physical level of the animals by their weakness for *carnall and foull delyte*, the desires of the flesh. Human life is a constant struggle to overcome our carnal instincts in favour of our spiritual qualities.

Praising the style of Aesop's writing (or that of Gualterus), Henryson repeats the reminder that his author wrote figuratively *Be figure*, and so introduces the first tale, that of the cock which found a pretty stone.

1 The Cock and the Jasp

The Taill of the Cok, and the Jasp

This seems at first sight to be a relatively short and simple fable, being the only one in which there is no interaction between animals. The main interest lies in the ambiguous relationship between the tale and its associated moralitas.

Basic story: A cock looking for food finds a precious stone instead, a jasp, and while acknowledging the value of the stone, he recognises that it has little use for him and immediately rejects it.

Since this fable is clearly intended to be the first of the thirteen (1.61) it may be seen to be establishing patterns of narrative and of interpretation which Henryson wishes to continue throughout the series. The structure is straightforward enough: two stanzas introduce the situation; in the following five the cock expatiates on his dilemma, and in a final stanza the narrator leads from the tale to the moralitas.

The impression given throughout by the cock is of modesty and commonsense; he contrasts the dignity of the stone

O gentill Iasp, O riche and nobill thing 79

with the degrading circumstances in which it is found *"in this mydding ... amang this muke and mold"*, and points out that although *"grit lordis"* might find a use for it, he himself would prefer to find some food

As draf or corne, small wormis, or snaillis,
Or ony meit wald do my stomok gude. 94–5

Indeed this idea of contrast between the stone's value and the cock's needs forms the basic structure of this part of the tale, and is expressed in the frequent antithetical form the lines take:

	Thocht I the find, thow ganis not for me	80
or:	Thow hes na corne, and thairof I had neid	99
or:	Thow ganis not for me, nor I for the.	112

Another noteworthy feature is the respect the cock expresses towards the jasp, which reaches its climax in the last spoken stanza, with three rhetorical questions:

Quhar suld thou mak thy habitatioun?
Quhar suld thow duell, bot in ane royall tour?
Quhar suld thow sit, bot on ane kingis croun
Exalt in worschip and in grit honour?   106–109

and ends with the reverential:

Rise, gentill Iasp, of all stanis the flour,
Out of this fen, and pas quhar thow suld be.   110–111

The narrator's move from tale to comment is intriguing; the stone is left upon the ground:

Bot quhen or how or quhome be it wes found
As now I set to hald na argument.   115–116

... only the first example we shall see of Henryson's conscious dismissiveness with incidental matters. He then turns to his interpretation:

Bot of the inward sentence and intent
Of this fabill, as myne author dois write,
I sall reheirs in rude and hamelie dite.   117–119

Moralitas

The conventional self-deprecation of the phrase "*rude and hamelie dite*" need not distract the reader from the perhaps unexpected line he takes in the moralitas. Three stanzas are used to extol the merits of the stone, and then, with a feeling of the argument being belatedly shifted, a particular property is specified:

This gentill iasp, richt different of hew,
Betakinnis perfite prudence and cunning.   127–8

Building his argument, he repeats the form of the triple rhetorical question used in the tale to hammer the point home:

> Quha may be hardie, riche and gratious?
> Quha can eschew perrell and auenture?
> Quha can gouerne ane realme, cietie, or hous
> Without science? No man, I ʒow assure.   134–137

Having established that the jasp is not to be taken as merely a valuable stone, but as a symbol of knowledge and learning, Henryson brings this interpretation to bear on the actions of the cock, with the severe comment:

> This cok, desyrand mair the sempill corne
> Than ony iasp, may till ane fule be peir ...   141–142

But such a judgement seems misdirected at the sensible cock, especially when line 156 makes it clear that even human beings "seik it nocht", and Henryson once again employs that expressively curt ending, leaving the moral decision to the reader:

> Ga seik the iasp, quha will, for thair it lay.   161

What exactly is going on here? It seems likely that the average reader of the tale will feel some sympathy with the cock, and be of the opinion that he is being encouraged to recognise the wisdom of the animal in not involving himself in matters outwith his realm, an idea which is the basis of the moralitas in both *The Two Mice* and in *The Wolf and the Wether*. That the reading of the moralitas usually comes as a surprise is not in question; so what is Henryson up to? It is not very likely that he is being careless; he is if anything a poet who takes a great deal of care in his work, and it is even less likely that the first of all his fables would not receive particular attention. Is it then a *deliberately* unexpected interpretation? It has been suggested that Henryson began his collection of fables with a simple tale, but eschewed the obvious interpretation in favour of forcing the reader to think more precisely about the issues, and making the reader alert to readings which might otherwise be taken on the nod. On the other hand, to take the moralitas at face value, it is consistent with the principles expounded in the course of the Fables as a whole to decry those who are blinded by material desires and who as a result neglect spiritual awareness. Whatever the reason, it is with a sense of heightened awareness, and some wariness, that the reader must pass on to the second fable.

2   The Two Mice

The Taill of the Uponlandis Mous, and the Burges Mous

One of the best known stories of Aesop, the tale of the Town
Mouse and the Country Mouse, this social satire on people who
get above themselves revolves largely round the amusingly
precise depiction of the two sisters and the touchiness of their
relationship, expressed largely by means of the dialogue.

Basic story: The Town Mouse goes to visit her sister in the
country, and being unhappy with the food she is given, invites her
to come to town. They eat well till they are frightened by the
arrival, first of the spenser or steward, then of the cat, who
attacks the country mouse. She escapes, and swears to go home
and never return to a place of such danger.

The social distinction between the two sisters is set out in the first
two stanzas, one sister living in poverty, hunger and cold, and the
other having status in society and access to as much food as she
requires. Henryson has much fun moving back and forward
between the worlds of human and animals, and describing the
Town Mouse in terms taken exclusively from the social and
commercial worlds of human beings:

> (She ...) Was gild brother and made ane fre burges,
> 　　Toll-fre als, but custum mair or les,　　　172–173

though it should be noted that Henryson has already, and much
more subtly, presented the Country Mouse in human terms, in the
casual use of the phrase:

> Quhilis in the corne, in vther mennis skaith　　167

... where the word *vther* includes the mouse in the world of
human affairs.

　　The Town Mouse's journey adopts many of the typical devices
associated with nature poetry: alliteration, the list, structural
repetition, and the use of standard phrases like *busk and breir*,
already used in line 166:

> Throw mony wilsum wayis can scho walk,
> Throw mosse and mure, throw bankis, busk and breir,
> Fra fur to fur, cryand fra balk to balk ...　　　183–5

When the sisters meet, their relationship is established first of all in the interesting line 190 by the narrator commenting explicitly on the *"hartlie cheir"*, deepened by the exclamation *"Lord God!"* and setting up at the same time a relationship between narrator and reader with *geue ȝe had sene* . The set of past tense verbs: *leuch, gret, kissit, plet* ... continues the delineation of the scene.

The narrator seems concerned to keep himself to the forefront at this stage with the little incidental phrases, or tags: *As I hard say* (197) and *I do it on thame besyde* (207)

The action properly begins with the distaste expressed by the Town Mouse. These few stanzas (lines 204–252) contain some very fine social humour, many of whose delicate strokes arise from the consciousness of difference in status between the sisters. First the burgess *prunȝit forth in pride* (208) and criticises the food which her sister has provided, but none of her preening is quite equal to the devastatingly ironic *Madame* with which the Country Mouse begins her reply. This word clearly indicates that she thinks her sister is getting above herself, and in the rest of that stanza she reminds her that they had the same lowly beginnings, and that she, at least, has kept to the customs they used to hold. The Town Mouse resumes the battle with the icily polite:

> My fair sister, quod scho, haue me excusit   218

and continues with

> Sister, this victuall and ȝour royall feist
> May weill suffice for sic ane rurall beist.   244–245

... where it is hard to say whether the sarcasm of *ȝour royall feist* is less or more offensive than the description of her sister as *sic ane rurall beist*. Their arrival in town brings them to a place of plenty:

> Baith cheis and butter vpon skelfis hie,
> Flesche and fische aneuch, baith fresche and salt,
> And sekkis full off grotis, meill and malt.   264–6

Again Henryson plays with our sense of the animals as partaking of both animal and human qualities when he underlines their arrival *Withowt God speid* and their dining *Withowtin grace*, and their eating and drinking like lords:

> Except ane thing: thay drank the watter cleir
> In steid off wyne.   272–3

In the midst of all their pleasure the narrator interjects a portentous adage which forewarns:

> 3it efter ioy oftymes cummis cair,
> And troubill efter grit prosperitie.   290–1

– a warning fulfilled by the unexpected arrival of the spenser. Their haste to escape from him is underlined by the ironic understatement of line 295, where again the narrator is seen to be explicitly controlling the reader's reactions:

> Thay taryit not to wesche, as I suppose.   295

It is clear that the Town Mouse is well accustomed to danger as is seen by the phrase *The bald burgess* (l.306) and in her insouciant invitation to dine in line 317. The spenser's brief appearance had given them only a fright; the arrival of the cat on the other hand presents actual danger, the physical nature of which is skilfully portrayed by the phrases *Fra fute to fute ... to and fra ... Quhylis vp, quhylis doun.*

When the Country Mouse has finally had enough, her disillusionment with her sister's hospitality is marked by the change from the formal *3ow / 3e / 3our,* which has been used till now, to the informal (and presumably more honest) *thy* in 344–7. As in the previous fable, the narrator makes an appearance again just before ending, where again there is a kind of detachment from responsibility for the tale in the deliberately vague phrases *I can not tell ... Bot I hard say ...*

Moralitas

Henryson immediately sets up an informal, cosy relationship between himself and the reader:

> Freindis, heir may 3e find, will 3e tak heid ...   365

> Thy awin fyre, freind ...   389

which he uses to attack, not the pride of the Town Mouse, but rather the presumption of the Country Mouse, though it is perhaps significant that the moralitas really bears little direct relationship to the tale; only the generalised warning:

> The cat cummis and to the mous hes ee   384

picks up any of the referents in the tale. The rest simply reiterates the highly conservative moral, underlined by the *small possessioun* refrain, that one should be happy with what one has.

3   The Cock and the Fox

The Taill of Schir Chantecleir and the Foxe

The first of the Reynardian tales in the collection; based on Chaucer's version in the *Nonne's Priest's Tale.*

Basic story: A hungry fox flatters a cock by saying that he knew the cock's father and so they should be friends; he challenges him to sing like his father and when the gullible cock relaxes his guard the fox grabs him and makes off. The cock's three hens talk about his apparent demise, revealing their true opinions. Finally the cock has an inspiration and escapes.

The first stanza states the basic premise of the fables, that each animal has a particular quality associated with it, and the fox is soon characterised by the use of phrases such as *craftie and cautelous*; *The ieperdies, the wayis and the wyle; begyle; dissimuland*. It has been remarked that when a fox falls to his knees in mediaeval literature, other animals should look to their safety; what may look like a suppliant or subservient posture is of course the fox engaged in stalking its prey. This is his first action here.

When he speaks to the cock he establishes their supposed relationship by the sycophantic tone of his language: *my maister; Schir*. Another technique he uses is to talk so much that the cock can say little in reply. The gullible cock asks only *Knew ʒe my father?* and the silly giggle which accompanies the question assures the fox that he has chosen his prey well. Adding the circumstantial evidence of the *birkin beuch* and the *Dirigie* (the first word of the office for the dead) to convince the cock of his presence at his father's death (one detail which is easy to believe!) he then moves into straightforward flattery, judging correctly that the cock is foolish enough to fall for it:

> Quhen I behald ʒour fedderis fair and gent,
> ʒour beik, ʒour breist, ʒour hekill, and ʒour kame ... 453–4

After his question about his father, the cock has only the single word *Quhat?* before he is grabbed and hurried off.

Much of the humour so far has arisen from the accuracy of portrayal of the machinations of the fox and the vanity of the cock. Henryson now employs another technique by which he expresses the result of this farmyard fracas in terms more suitable for an Homeric struggle. The widow's reaction to the loss of her cock:

> As sho wer woid, with mony ʒell and cry,
> Ryuand hir hair, vpon hir breist can beit;
> Syne paill off hew, half in ane extasy,
> Fell doun for cair in swoning and in sweit.   488–491

is expressed by the device known as Mock Epic, which is used to describe a trivial or local affair in terms more appropriate to serious matters, and is continued when Henryson, telling how the hens reacted, uses the highly legalistic term that they:

> Fell of that cace in disputatioun.   494

Henryson gives more attention to this section than Chaucer did, providing three hens rather than Chaucer's one, and the Mock Epic is carried on in Pertok's speech, not only by the elaborate metaphors used for the cock:

> Our nichtingall, and als our orlege bell   498

but also by the device of rhetorical question:

> Quha sall our lemman be? Quha sall vs leid?
> Quhen we ar sad quha sall vnto vs sing?   502–3

The three hens are differentiated by their reactions to Chantecleir's abduction, and it seems at first that Pertok feels only grief, but Henryson has mischievously included the remark, when praising Chantecleir's lovemaking:

> In paramouris he wald do vs plesing   506

and then adds the devastatingly deflating:

> At his power, as nature list him geif.   507

The second hen, Sprutok, has no doubts about her reaction; she will dress in her best clothes and sing the song: *Wes neuer wedow sa gay!*

Sprutok reminds Pertok of the cock's limitations, including his sexual failings:

> Off chalmerglew, Pertok, full weill ʒe knaw
> Waistit he wes, off nature cauld and dry.   518–9

With Sprutok's example before her, Pertok now speaks her true mind: she will find a better lover than Chantecleir within the week. The third hen, Coppok, recounting Chantecleir's sins, sees a sign of God's judgement in his demise. The cock's self-satisfaction is thereby shown to be unjustified.

When the widow sends her dogs after the fox their journey is expressed in alliterative phrases, like the Town Mouse's:

> With that, but baid, they braidet ouer the bent;
> As fyre off flint thay ouer the feildis flaw;
> Full wichtlie thay throw wood and wateris went ...   551–3

The arrival of the dogs worries the fox and from somewhere the cock gets a good idea; he is *with sum gude spirit inspyrit,* and makes his escape. The didactic purpose of the fables is further underlined when Henryson, in the middle of the narrative, inserts a piece of proverbial wisdom:

> For falset failʒeis ay at the latter end   568

(a saying which is used in similarly sanctimonious circumstances at line 1997.)

The balance of the dialogue has now shifted in favour of the cock, who speaks at far greater length than earlier, while the fox is reduced to impotent pleading. As he nears the end of the narrative, Henryson reasserts the role of the narrator again with the words *Now iuge ʒe all* 571; the cock has learned his lesson.

Moralitas
Again, Henryson begins by setting up an amicable relationship with the readers: *worthie folk; gude folk,* then reverts to the defence of his fable by asserting that there is *ane sentence richt agreabill.*

This is one of the fables where he attempts to work out a more complete system of analogies, whereby elements in the fable represent other things in the real world. His equation of the jasp with knowledge has been noted; no similar equation was offered in *The Two Mice,* but now:

> To our purpose this cok weill may we call
> Nyse proud men   590–1

and:

> This fenʒeit foxe may weill be figurate
> To flatteraris.   600–1

It is interesting to note that the hens, perhaps being instruments of humour rather than of instruction, are not represented in the moralitas.

The straightforward final lesson, then is: avoid pride and flattery.

4   The Fox and the Wolf

The Taill how this foirsaid Tod maid his Confession to Freir Wolf Waitskaith

With this fable we enter a world of hilarious knockabout humour on the one hand, and on the other, of deceit, violence and retribution. The combination of the two elements gives most of the Reynardian fables their particular texture.

Basic story: The same fox as in the previous fable has a prevision of his miserable end, and to avert it decides to confess his sins to a wolf in the form of *Ane worthie doctour of divinitie*. The fox flatters the wolf who agrees to hear his confession. Although the fox can't make a genuine confession, he is nonetheless granted absolution; no sooner is he absolved from sin than he kills a kid, baptises it as a salmon and eats it. When resting, he muses that it would be fitting if he were to be killed by an arrow at that moment; that is then what happens!

The fable begins with a very clear link to the previous one, making it obvious that we are dealing with the same fox. Something of the manner in which Henryson gains our sympathy, at least in part, for the fox can be seen in his evident *joie de vivre*:

> Than Lourence luikit vp, quhair he couth ly,
> And kest his hand vpon his ee on hicht,
> Merie and glad that cummit wes the nicht.   625–7

From his observation of the heavens he recognises that his sinful life will lead him to a sticky end, and determines to seek a confessor to whom he might confess his sins. On cue comes Freir Wolf Waitskaith, the wolf's grey coat perhaps suggesting the grey habit of the friar. The reader should be alerted to the fox's real intentions, however, by three hints which Henryson gives: his narratorial comment on the fox's nature (*this wylie tratour tod*), the fox's immediate demeanour (*On kneis fell* ... and we remember that this was the manner in which he approached the cock in the previous fable ... *with mony binge and mony beck*,) and the fox's own flattering and self-deprecating words, which are just too reminiscent of the words he had addressed to the cock:

> Ʒe ar the lanterne and the sicker way
> Suld gyde sic sempill folk as me to grace.   677–8

Similarly, the wolf's little chuckle on line 684 (*and leuch*) is expressed in exactly the same words as the cock's smug giggle on line 446.

Before launching into the parody of the sacrament of confession which follows, Henryson underlines the sanctity of confession by having his narrator move discreetly aside from their conversation, lest he overhear anything said under the seal of the confessional. This of course does not prevent him from giving a verbatim report of the conversation! The "confession" itself is a clear demonstration of the fox's devious intent; three elements are necessary for a "good" confession: genuine contrition, renunciation of the sin, and the acceptance of an appropriate penance. The fox fails to comply with any of these requirements, saying that he repents only of having killed so few hens and lambs, and that he needs to continue doing so in order to live. With a reluctant *Weill* ... (a device Henryson uses several times when a slow-witted wolf is not quite able to put his finger on where precisely he is being tricked) the wolf passes over these first two requirements:

> To the thrid part off pennance let vs ga   714

– whereupon the fox claims that he is too weak to accept any heavy penance. The wolf orders him to give up meat till Easter, and instead of accepting this meekly, the fox begins to negotiate as many exceptions as he can get away with:

> I grant thairto, swa ʒe will giff me leif
> To eit puddingis, or laip ane lyttill blude,
> Or heid, or feit, or paynchis let me preif   726–8

and is given permission to eat meat twice a week in case of great need.

The fox heads for the river, intending to catch fish, but very soon recognises his unfitness for that occupation, and spying a flock of goats, he manages to make off with a kid. The parody of confession is now followed by a monstrous, and yet funny, parody of the sacrament of baptism. Acknowledging that the kid is meat, he takes the animal to the water and submerges it, with the memorable words:

> Ga doun, schir Kid, cum vp, Schir Salmond, agane   751

by which means he renames the kid and reclassifies it as fish, under which heading it may be eaten with impunity! The breathtaking audacity of the fox in reshaping the world to his own requirements has something admirable in it, the gallusness of a streetfighter, which causes the reader to have mixed feelings about his inevitable end. Henryson's humour involves generating some sympathy for the rogue, so that we feel with him his self-satisfaction when he stretches himself out to digest, with the fateful words:

> Vpon this wame set wer ane bolt full meit   760

that is to say something like, "It would just be typical if I were shot by an arrow now!"

Inevitably, the keeper of the goats then shoots him with an arrow, but instead of ending the tale with the immediate death of the fox, Henryson permits him such wryly fatalistic and psychologically realistic last words, that all can sympathise:

> Me think na man may speik ane word in play
> Bot now on dayis in ernist it is tane.   770–1

It should be observed, however, that in immediate juxtaposition to the black humour of these remarks is the uncompromising violence of the dead fox being skinned in recompense for the kid.

Moralitas

The short moralitas which follows provides the expected interpretation: the sudden death of the fox is a warning to us all; some people cannot repent because they enjoy their sins, some cannot give up their sins because they are accustomed to them, but sudden death may take any of us. Finally, Henryson reiterates the three points necessary for a proper confession:

> Ceis of ȝour sin; remord ȝour conscience;
> Do wilfull penance here.   793–4

5   The Trial of the Fox

The Taill of the Son & Air of the foirsaid Foxe, callit Father wer: Alswa the Parliament of fourfuttit Beistis, haldin be the Lyoun.

This fable allows Henryson to show what he can do in one of the traditional devices of mediaeval poetry: the elaborately formalised list, here of animals in attendance at the court. The splendour of the Lion's parliament is contrasted with the slapstick violence attending the fox and wolf.

Basic story: The son of the fox in the previous fable is glad to find
the skinned corpse of his father, since he will now inherit his
territory; he discards the body unceremoniously. When this has
been done, he hears a unicorn blow a bugle and, as herald, read a
summons to all animals from King Lion to attend a parliament.
The Lion declares the magnificence of his peace. Fearing justice,
the fox tries to hide. Only a mare is absent from the assembly; the
fox and the wolf are sent to fetch her. The mare claims that she
possesses an exemption and invites them to read it; the fox, ever
reluctant to enmesh himself in potential difficulties, says he can't
read, so the wolf is inveigled into doing it. When the wolf goes to
read he is kicked by the mare. While off to fetch water to wash
blood from the wolf's face the fox sees a troop of lambs and
opportunistically kills and eats the fattest.

Back in court, the fox gets all the animals to laugh at the wolf's
injuries. Just at this point the ewe, the dead lamb's mother, enters
and accuses the fox of the killing; he is swiftly tried and hanged.

The first phrase of the fable *This forsaid foxe* links it to the
previous one, and introduces the son of that fox, known as *Father-
war* (worse than his father!) His amorality is demonstrated by his
thanking God for his father's death and by his casual disposal of
the body. (In that context, note the irony of line 824: *throw
naturall pietie!*) With his character thus established, the tale
proper can begin with the arrival of the unicorn, who reads the
summons *To brutall beistis and irrationall* (857) to attend the
Lion's parliament.

The formal list was a standard set-piece of mediaeval poetry,
found also for example in *The Kingis Quair*, and here Henryson
provides legendary and heraldic creatures like the minotaur (half-
man, half-bull) and Pegasus (the winged horse) along with the
everyday animals of the countryside:

> The da, the ra, the hornit hart, the hynd   900

and the lowly creatures like *the lytill mous*. The lion's address to
the animals, stressing his power and mercy and the security of his
peace, is sometimes seen as a recognition by Henryson of the
growing power of the throne in fifteenth-century Scotland, and
ends with a reference to lambs being safe from foxes when the lion
is near, a remark which the fox takes personally, believing that he
is about to be punished for his misdeeds. Henryson interposes two
stanzas of moralistic condemnation of the fox's falsehood (lines
971–984) perhaps as a necessary counterpoint to the possibility of

the reader's siding with the fox for his ingenuity. When the fox is
singled out to fetch the mare, his instant reaction is to seek a
means of avoiding the task, by pleading disablement, and impli-
cating the wolf instead:

> Aa, schir, mercie! Lo, I haue bot ane ee,
> Hurt in the hoche, and cruikit as ȝe may se.
> The volff is better in ambassatry
> And mair cunning in clergie fer than I.   995–8

and in the end the lion sends both of them. We are once again in
the territory of the wily fox and the gullible wolf, and again the
fox demurs in any situation of risk, cheerfully presenting the wolf
as a far more suitable ambassador:

> I can not spell, quod he, sa God me speid.
> Heir is the volff, ane nobill clerk at all,
> And of this message is maid principall.   1011–2

When the wolf is kicked so hard by the mare that he lies *Halff out
off lyif*, it is hard not to feel once more a measure of admiration for
the quick-thinking fox, whose *Schadenfreude* at the wolf's
discomfiture is so wryly expressed in the use of Latin, both in
Lupus, thow art loist and in the proverb on line 1033. Henryson
offsets any such admiration, however, and makes a point of
reasserting the moral world when the killing of the lamb is
immediately preceded not by the amusing behaviour of the fox,
but by the narrator's pointing the reader in the direction he
wishes us to take: the fox is called *fraudfull*, indeed, he is:

> This tratour tod, this tirrant, and this tyke.   1045

Back at the parliament, the fox again is allowed to demonstrate
his agility of wit when he causes the entire assembly to laugh at
the wolf's broken head, mocking him with its resemblance to the
clergyman's red hat, but just as he seems to be winning the court
round, nemesis appears in the form of the mother of the murdered
lamb, seeking justice. Even in the face of death the fox attempts to
wriggle out of it with an ingenious excuse, that he had only meant
to play with the lamb, who killed himself in his rush to escape,
but the evidence: *the woll, the fleeche, ȝit stikkis on thy teith* is
conclusive. The consequence is an instant trial and hanging. Once
again the violent humour is brought to an end by a speedy and
unprepared death. It might be mentioned at this point that
Henryson has so accustomed us to his world of human characteristics expressed through the medium of animals that it no longer

seems in any way odd that not only do other animals arraign and condemn a fox, but they *tak off all his clais*, and subject him to a judicial hanging.

Moralitas

The first stanza deals yet again with the seriousness possible with poetry:

> Richt so vnder ane fabill figurall
> Sad sentence men may seik.   1099–1100

Perhaps surprisingly Henryson's analogies then present the lion, not as king, but as the world, in the sense of worldly distractions,

> To quhome loutis (*bows*) baith empriour and king.   1105

The mare, being exempt from attendance on the lion, represents therefore *men of contemplatioun ... Abstractit from this warldis wretchitnes*. The wolf, the compliant servant of the world, is sensuality (severely injured by men of contemplation) and the fox, having been sent to summon men of contemplation back to the world, at the command of worldliness (perhaps less convincingly, given the assiduity with which he tried to avoid the task) represents temptation. The last stanza is one of the few pieces of earlier writing which has survived the post-reformation expunging of references to the Virgin Mary, or modifications to comply with the reformed religion.

6   The Sheep and the Dog

The Taill of the Scheip and the Doig

A tale of institutionalised injustice, with a moralitas which is unusual in that the main character appears again and continues the action.

Basic story: A dog summons a sheep to court to win back a piece of bread; the court is packed with the sheep's enemies, who, in spite of her eloquent pleading and the justice of her plea, find against her and she is forced to sell her fleece to pay for the bread.

Henryson's stark tale of the abuse of justice and the practice of bearing false witness may be seen as a comment on the corruption of the courts in his own day, though as ever, its application is universal. The reader is given clear directions as to the intended interpretation. The wolf is immediately introduced as *fraudfull*, and we are informed that the raven *pykit had full mony scheipis ee*, while by contrast, the sheep is described as *selie* (innocent or wretched). It is stressed that the court is being held at an unlawful time (*Quhen Hesperus to schaw his face began*) and the court is staffed by officials who are predators: the wolf, the raven, the fox, the gled, the graip. Henryson's legal expertise appears to advantage in this fable, not least in the irony of the sheep's using legal means to defend himself, by eloquently denying the authority and competence of the court:

> Heir I declyne the iuge, the tyme, the place.   1187

The narrator conducts the reader through the arbitration with ironic asides: *I schrew thame ay that leis ... On clerkis I do it*, till the court finds for the dog, which has been treated in a relatively neutral manner until now, when it becomes *this fals doig*. Henryson's narrator openly sides with the sheep:

> Off this sentence, allace, quhat sall I say,
> Quhilk dampnit hes the selie innocent,
> And iustifit the wrangous iugement?   1248–50

and the final stanza depicting the sheep complying with the unjust sentence further inclines the reader to the sheep's cause by the bleakness of its last line:

> Naikit and bair syne to the feild couth pas.   1257

Moralitas

The sheep, not surprisingly, represent the common people who are subject to the cruelties of tyrants; interesting detail is supplied about the manner in which the wolf as a corrupt sheriff extracts payment from the poor and how the raven alters names in return for bribes and so forth. The really unusual part of this moralitas comes from the resumption of the action of the fable, where the narrator *as I passit by* overhears the sheep's complaint. This begins by stressing the physical hardships of winter which the shorn sheep must suffer, insistently drawing God's attention by means of the imperative verbs *Walk ... discerne ... Se how ... Se how ...* and goes on to demand of God why he permits abuses like covetousness and simony, but the sheep concludes by answering the question himself by likening these sufferings to the other sufferings which God sends:

> Thow sendis vs troubill and plaigis soir,
> As hunger, derth, grit weir, or pestilence   1315-6

and which *sen that we ar opprest / In to this eirth*, are part of the human condition, admitting of no resolution on this side of heaven.

7 The Lion and the Mouse

The Taill of the Lyon & the Mous

This fable plays a particularly interesting part in the cycle, being the central fable numerically, and is seemingly marked out by Henryson not only by having a Prologue of its own, but by the appearance of Aesop himself, who ostensibly tells the tale, and who is asked by the glamour-stricken narrator to supply the moralitas.

Basic story: This is the well-known tale of the lion who was merciful to the mouse he found running over him, and who was later rescued by the sharp teeth of mice after being caught in a net; it is an ideal basis for exploration of the themes of justice, mercy and the proper use of power.

The importance Henryson attaches to this fable is further marked by its having an opening which is more common in larger scale, more ambitious works, such as Dunbar's *The Golden Targe,* and bears many of the features of such works: the opening in early summer; the classical appellation of the sun god; the alliterative description of nature; the narrator going alone into the countryside; the flowers, the birds, the dream.

   In his dream Aesop appears to him, carrying paper, pen and inkhorn, and identifies himself, incidentally implying that Henryson believed him to be a Roman. When besought to tell a tale, Aesop reiterates the usual objection:

> For quhat is it worth to tell ane fenȝeit taill,
> Quhen haly preiching may na thing auaill?   1389-90

Nonetheless, he accedes to the narrator's repeated request and tells of the sleeping lion who is wakened by the mice running over his body and captures *the maister mous* who first attempts to excuse itself by claiming that they had thought the lion was dead.

This may be taken as an implicit criticism of the lion, for failing to perform his ordained role. When the lion refuses to accept this as a valid excuse, the mouse makes an eloquent and lengthy appeal to the lion's sense of his own honour and dignity:

> It will degraid sum part of ʒour renoun
> To sla ane mous, quhilk may mak na defence
> Bit askand mercie at ʒour excellence. 1486–8

The appeal is successful, and the lion releases the mouse and goes off hunting; it is significant that the picture of his hunting is not flattering; he is called *This cruell lyoun*, and:

> ... slew baith tayme and wyld, as he wes wont,
> And in the cuntrie maid ane grit deray. 1512–3

Eventually he is captured himself, and delivers a formal lamentation bewailing his plight:

> O lamit lyoun, liggand heir sa law ... 1531

The mouse hears his lament, summons the other mice and releases the lion. We are reminded that Aesop himself is the teller of this tale when the wide-eyed narrator asks:

> "Maister, is thair ane moralitie
> In this fabill? 1570–1

– and indeed there is.

Moralitas

The lion is a ruler who neglects his people, the forest is the material world with all its evanescent attractions (we may remember that the lion stood for the world and its distractions in *The Trial of the Fox.*) The mice are the common people, but the essential point is that they require the constant *correctioun* of their rulers or they will *misknaw* those who are in authority over them, and so act out of their station, that constantly nagging fear felt by the rulers in any static society. The need for mercy in administration is stressed, as is the desirability of prudence, which links this fable to the next. It has been suggested that the choice of this story, and the lines:

> Mair till expound, as now, I lett allane,
> Bot king and lord may weill wit quhat I mene:
> Figure heirof oftymis hes bene sene. 1612–4

may refer directly to specific events in Henryson's own time. The lion might then be seen as a representation of James III, and his capture a reference to his difficulties with over-mighty nobles, all discreetly mediated through the persona of Aesop. Whether or not this is the case, Henryson has Aesop conclude with a valedictory exhortation which hands control back to the narrator:

> And with that word he vanist and I woke;
> Syne throw the schaw my iourney hamewart tuke.   1620–1

8   The Preaching of the Swallow

The Preiching of the Swallow

One of the most remarkable of the fables, both in its lengthy and significant introduction, and in the urgency communicated by the swallow.

Basic story: The narrator overhears a swallow in the spring warning the other birds that the fowler is growing seed to make nets for them; the birds scorn the swallow's advice. Then in June the swallow shows them that the seed is now already growing; the birds ignore his warnings. The harvest comes and the nets are made; in winter the little birds seek shelter in the fowler's barn and haystacks; he throws out chaff for them as a trap and they are tricked. The fowler takes them and brutally kills them; the swallow flies off.

The lengthy and complex introduction of thirteen stanzas marks this fable as bearing particular significance. The first four stanzas (ll.1622–1649) deal with the greatness of God and our weak understanding of His greatness, ending with the very mediaeval injunction:

> Nane suld presume be ressoun naturall
> To seirche the secreitis off the Trinitie,
> Bot trow fermelie and lat all ressoun be.   1647–9

God's greatness nevertheless may be perceived by the splendour of his creation, as in the flowers, the firmament, the four elements of :

> The fyre, the air, the watter, and the ground.   1661

Similarly, the fish in the sea, the beasts on the earth, the birds in the air, and above all man, his last creation, demonstrate God's greatness. Illustrating the cycle of the year, Henryson provides traditionally alliterative descriptions of the four seasons, starting with summer, giving each season a single stanza, except winter, which gets two, perhaps in acknowledgement of the Scottish literary tradition of writing about winter, or perhaps recognising how the winter dominates the Scottish year! Finally spring appears, and with spring comes the narrator, walking forth on a May morning, simply for the delight of watching the activity in the fields, and the narrative begins. On three occasions, in spring, in June and in winter, the narrator recounts the behaviour of the birds. On the first occasion (lines 1713–1775) he overhears the swallow's warning to the other birds, couched in remarkably urgent terms, an urgency which is given to the poem by the insistent repetition of the word *se*, four examples of the demonstrative *ʒone*, and the exclamatory *lo.* :

> 'Se ʒe ʒone churll', quod scho, 'beʒond ʒone pleuch
> Fast sawand hemp – lo se! – and linget seid?'   1743–4

His very physical instructions:

> ... and with our naillis scharp and small
> Out of the eirth scraip we ʒone seid anone
> And eit it vp,   1749–51

are concluded by an elegant Latin quotation and a rather more abstract dissertation on prudence. The lack of foresight of the birds is emphasised by their complacent citing of proverbs in response to the immediacy of the swallow's urging:

> 'The barne is eith to busk that is vnborne;
> Al growis nocht that in the ground is set;
> The nek to stoup quhen it the straik sall get
> Is sone aneuch; deith on the fayest fall.'
> This scornit thay the swallow ane and all.   1764–8

The second sighting of the birds (lines 1776–1824) is introduced by the narrator commenting on the ominous growth of the seeds, which now, in June:

> Wer growin hie, that hairis mycht thame hyde.   1778

The urgency of the swallow is again emphasised, this time principally by the imperative verbs by which he tries to force the birds to take action: *Lift vp ... Luke to ... Go ʒit ... pull it vp ... let it na mair incres!* This episode is again marked off by the narrator going home. Particularly worth looking at is the stanza starting at line 1825 which gives a detailed account of the manufacture of nets, from the ripening of the lint, and therefore covering the period of autumn. Then winter comes on, with its customary alliterative force:

> The wynter come, the wickit wind can blaw,
> The woddis grene wer wallowit with the weit,
> Baith firth and fell with froistys wer maid faw,
> Slonkis and slaik maid slidderie with the sleit.   1832–5

The final sighting of the birds (though the narrator is only implicitly present according to line 1874 and the last line) runs from line 1832 to the end of the fable, The swallow's final warning again begins in urgency, with exclamations, rhetorical question and imperative verbs:

> 'Into that calf scraip quhill ȝour naillis bleid—
> Thair is na corne, ȝe labour all in vane.
> Trow ȝe ȝone churll for pietie will ȝow feid?
> Na, na, he hes it heir layit for ane trane.
> Remoue, I reid, or ellis ȝe will be slane ... '   1854

followed by a more formalised repetitive moralising (*Grit fule is he* ...). The violence of the end of the birds is underlined by alliteration:

> That bludie bowcheour beit thay birdis doun   1875

and by the physical movements and concrete nouns:

> Sum with ane staf he straik to eirth on swoun,
> Off sum the heid, off sum he brak the crag,
> Sum half on lyfe he stoppit in his bag.   1878–80

Moralitas

While Henryson makes the by now familiar plea for tolerance of the fable on the grounds that it *may weill be applicate / To gude morall edificatioun*, he underlines the perceived relative triviality of the fable by stating that Aesop wrote it

> Quhen that he waikit from mair autentik werk   1890

and proceeds to elucidate the *sentence*.

The analogies are satisfyingly convincing in this fable: the fowler is the devil setting his nets to entrap the unwary; the chaff is the worthlessness of material possessions; temptation is the seed which grows into sin. The birds are wretches blinded by these material possessions, and the swallow is of course the preacher, ever warning of the devil's traps. Henryson modulates very skilfully from the story of the birds to its human application when he personalises the fate of the birds, asking the reader to apply it to himself:

> Quhat help is than this calf, thir gudis vane,
> Quhen thow art put in Luceferis bag,
> And brocht to hell, and hangit be the crag?   1934–6

Prudence and foresight are essential because of the uncertainty of human life, and so we must pray for four things: to give up sin; to give up dissension; to practise charity; to join the angels in bliss.

9   The Fox, the Wolf and the Cadger

The Taill of the Wolf that gat the Nekhering throw the wrinkis of the Foxe that begylit the Cadgear

A tale of trickery and violence as fox beguiles wolf again.

Basic story: A fox who is reluctantly in the service of a wolf devises a plan to cheat a cadger (pedlar) of his fish: he plays dead, and the cadger picks him up and throws him on the cart among the fish, which he throws to the wolf and then escapes. The wolf later tries the same trick, but the cadger is alert to it and beats him mercilessly.

The first eleven stanzas present a rather edgy negotiation between the wolf and the fox in which the fox continually demurs when it is suggested that he could be a successful hunter for the wolf. Their relative positions are marked by the wolf addressing the fox with the informal *thow / the / thy* while Lowrence uses the more respectful *ʒe / ʒour*. Each suggestion made by the wolf is met with the obsequious *'Schir,' said the foxe*, followed by his attempt to excuse himself. When the wolf angrily claims to be conscious of all the fox's wiles, the fox senses danger and diplomatically goes along with his wishes, denying (of course) any evil intent:

> I did bot till assay quhat ʒe wald say.   2016

The appearance of the cadger with his load of herring galvanises the fox into intrigue. The dialogue of the earlier stanzas, between the brutal directness of the wolf and the devious self-exoneration of the fox, is now succeeded by the fox being given seventeen successive lines to speak, packed with logical twists and turns, marked by *Thairfoir ... Sen ... Thocht ... Bot ... Giff ... For ...* in which he devises his plan as he goes, allocating parts and manipulating his supposed master presumably too quickly for the slow-witted wolf even to comment upon. The plan works well until the cadger notices what is going on and the fox runs off, mocking the man and his offered bait of the *nekhering* (the best fish, prominently displayed). With clear implications for what is to happen, the cadger, expressing his regret that he had no club to beat the fox with, breaks off a holly bough.

The wolf meanwhile has been impressed by the fox's feat, to which the fox does not fail to draw attention:

> 'Schir,' said he than, 'maid I not fair defend?'   2107

but puts himself into the fox's power by asking what the cadger had called out. Seeing his chance, the fox describes the nekhering in tempting terms designed to ensnare the sensuous wolf:

> It is ane syde of salmond, as it wair,
> And callour, pypand lyke ane pertrik ee.   2126–7

The wolf, by now well enmeshed, digs himself in further:

> Than said the volff, 'Quhat counsel geuis thou me?'   2130

and receives only too precise instructions from the fox to do as he had done, sometimes in the same words:

> First, ȝe man cast ane cumpas far about,
> Syne straucht ȝou doun in middis off the way.   2133–4
>   (& cf.2049–50)

Just as the fox in *The Cock and the Fox* used the *Dirigie* (the first word of the Office for the Dead) to cozen the wolf, this fox offers to say *In principio* (the first words of St. John's gospel) as an utterly spurious guarantee of good luck.

The cadger, who as we and the fox know is only too aware of this trick of playing dead, is not to be caught out twice, and beats him mercilessly, to the fox's great amusement:

> The foxe beheld that seruice quhair he lay,
> And leuch on loft quhen he the volff sa seis,
> Baith deif and dosinnit, fall swonand on his kneis.   2186–8

Henryson concludes by observing that the fox has managed to trick both the wolf and the man.

Moralitas

Somewhat over-defensively perhaps, in view of the undisciplined violence of the tale, Henryson asserts immediately that:

This taill is myngit with moralitee   2203

but his analogies fit fairly neatly, in fact: the fox represents the world with all its temptations, the wolf a man, only too impressionable and desiring material things, in turn represented by the herring which is like *the gold sa reid*. The cadger is Death, who comes when we least expect. The moralitas is then almost identical in purport to that of *The Preaching of the Swallow*, however different the tone of the two fables.

10 The Fox, the Wolf and the Husbandman

The Taill of the Foxe, that begylit the Wolf, in the schadow of the Mone

Once again the fox beguiles both wolf and man.

Basic story: A man ploughing with young oxen curses them for their inexperience by saying that the wolf might have them. Unknown to him, both wolf and fox are lying nearby and on his way home the wolf challenges him over the ownership of the team, calling the fox as witness. As ever, the fox turns the situation to his own advantage, striking a deal with each separately, promising the man his oxen in return for a few hens, and persuading the wolf to give up his claim in return for a cheese, which he tells the wolf can be found at the bottom of a well. In a short while the wolf is stuck at the bottom of the well while the fox makes his escape.

Henryson's fresh and affecting picture of the husbandman at work should be noted. The man's fear of the wolf, as well as being specified in his wish to retreat (1.2258) in his being *"sumdeill agast"* and in his *"felloun fray"* is strikingly seen in the address each uses to the other: the wolf disparagingly calls him *Carll*, while he respectfully uses the term *Schir* each time he speaks to the wolf. The man's last hope goes when the wolf calls Lowrence to witness, but the fox sees his chance and asks to be accepted by both as an arbiter. His devious approach to the man (*Freind ...*) and his suggestion that a small bribe might keep him his oxen, rings only too true. The atmosphere of amoral intrigue is strengthened by Lowrence's remark:

> For God is gane to sleip, as for this nycht.   2332

Having settled with the harmless man, the fox turns to the altogether more hazardous task of cheating the wolf, claiming that the man had offered a cheese for his oxen. The gormless but dangerous wolf puts himself in the fox's hands by asking:

> Is that thy counsell ... ?   2357

It should be noticed that the fox swears by his soul in reply (always a sure sign of bad faith, as when the other fox did in *The Cock and the Fox*, line 455), and demands:

> Schir, trow ȝe not I haue a saull to keip?   2363

Asking the fox's advice was the first sign of giving way, compounded by his grudging:

> 'Weill', quod the volff, 'it is aganis my will'   2364

and finally by his demand to see the cheese. The section which follows is a wonderfully humorous picture of the fox leading the wolf over the countryside *hand in hand*, while frantically trying to think how he might produce a cheese out of nowhere, till finally he gets an idea:

> Ȝit at the last he findis furth ane wyle,
> Than at him selff softlie couth he smyle.   2381–2

and shows the wolf the reflection of the moon in a well. One cannot but admire the fox's resourcefulness and quickness of wit when he forestalls any question about why on earth a cheese would be found down a well with:

> He hang it ȝonder that na man suld it steill.   2396

The knockabout action of this section is among the best in the fables, when the wolf tells Lowrence to get into one of the buckets and go down to fetch the cheese. Once down inside the well, the fox claims that the cheese is too heavy, and implores the wolf to come down in the other. Inevitably:

The tod come hailland vp, the volff ȝeid doun   2415

and Henryson presents a hilarious picture of the cheated wolf querulously demanding why he is on his way down as the crafty fox shoots past him up to the surface again, sanctimoniously ascribing their respective fates to the remorseless workings of the wheel of fortune. Perhaps because the humour has been so blatant, the poet feels the need to assure us in the last lines of the fable proper:

> Ȝyt men may find ane gude moralitie
> In this sentence, thocht it ane fabill be.   2425–6

Moralitas

This moralitas is one of the several places where it is suspected that some revision of Henryson's original text must have taken place in the sixteenth century, to make it conform to the principles of the new faith, and this is the likely explanation for some lack of clarity in the analogy he draws.

The wolf may very well stand for a wicked oppressor of the poor, the fox bears many of the features of the devil, the husbandman can easily be seen as a type of the godly man, and even the cheese may pass as a model for covetousness, but one balks somewhat at:

> The hennis ar warkis that fra ferme faith proceidis 2437

– when these same hens were the bribes given to the fox by the husbandman to allow him to keep his oxen! Similarly, there is a touch of contrivance about the equation of hell and the well:

> Christ keip all Christianis from that wickit well!   2454

It is not very likely that the reader will remember this somewhat laboured moralitas rather than the rumbustious humour of the tale itself.

11 The Wolf and the Wether

The Taill of the Wolf and the Wedder

The well-intentioned wether is ruthlessly slain by the wolf.

Basic story: A shepherd's dog which had protected his flock dies suddenly, leaving the shepherd grieving and wondering how to keep off the predators. A wether (a ram) offers to do the job with the skin of the old dog sewn on his back, and is very successful in frightening away all wild beasts. When a wolf takes a lamb the wether gives chase, bravely following the wolf until his false skin is ripped off by a brier bush and the wolf turns on him and after expressing his indignation, breaks his neck.

The first impressions of the wether are of a brave and resourceful animal; it approaches its master *wichtlie*, has a scheme fully worked out, and is highly praised by the shepherd for so doing:

'This come of ane gude wit:
Thy counsall is baith sicker, leill, and trew;
Quha sayis ane scheip is daft, thay lieit of it.'   2490–2

He successfully protects the flock, and when the *hungrie volff* appears, the wether does not hesitate, but *followit fast*. Even when the wolf discards the lamb to run the better, the wether is not distracted:

'Na,' quod the wedder, 'in faith we part not swa:
It is not the lamb, bot the, that I desyre ... '   2534–5

There is however, something risible and foolhardy as well as admirable in his remorseless pursuit of a wolf, to the extent that the wolf *for fleidnes fylit the feild*, and the moment of revelation, when *ane breir busk raif rudelie off the skyn* restores the true balance of power between the animals. However serious the matter may be for the wether, there is amusement to be had in the wolf's incredulous reaction, expressed in the numerous questions by which he tries to convince himself of the truth and by his outrage at the indignities to which he was subjected:

Thryis, be my saull, 3e gart me schute behind.   2567

The wether now in supplication addresses the wolf as *Maister* and *Schir*, and uses the formal second person, instead of the informal *the* which he had used in line 2535, quoted above, and in the following line. The wolf, presumably still in indignant shock, continues to employ the formal style, until the final stanza, when he reverts to the use of the informal *thy/thow*, an appropriate tone of address for one he is about to kill. A violent death brings all humour to an end.

Moralitas

The moralitas calls to mind that of *The Two Mice*: *riches of array* can cause the poor to become presumptuous; everyone should know his place in society,

> And fall not with thair better in debait,
> Suppois thay be als galland in thair geir   2611–2

– and as with the cock in *The Cock and the Jasp*, while we may recognise the validity of the interpretation, there remains a feeling that the positive qualities of bravery, loyalty and endurance manifested by the wether have been discounted.

12 The Wolf and the Lamb

The Taill of the Wolf and the Lamb

The simplest assertion of *force majeure*, the brutal assertion of might, without regard to morality.

Basic story: When a wolf and a lamb drink from the same stream, the wolf takes the opportunity of accusing the lamb of dirtying the water. The trouble the lamb takes in presenting a considered defence is seen to be useless when the wolf accuses the lamb's father of similar misdeeds; the lamb cites Scripture in his defence and demands a fair trial, but the wolf takes him and kills him.

Henryson sets up the opposition between the two animals from the start, where the wolf is introduced as:

> Ane cruell vollf, richt rauenous and fell   2616

and the lamb is *ane selie lamb* (2620). As well as addressing the lamb as *Thow catiue wretchit thing*, the wolf, as we might expect, uses the informal *thow / thy / the* while the lamb employs the more formal *ʒe, ʒour*, as well as the title *Schir*. The lamb's painstakingly precise defence, couched in language carefully designed to placate (*with ʒour leif ... Suppois*) is based on the seemingly undeniable fact that water may not run uphill, and ends with what is presented as an incontrovertible conclusion: *Ergo, ...* (2650) The wolf simply ignores this argument entirely and asserts the Old Testament reasoning that the lamb must suffer for his father's misdeeds. The lamb's pleading Christian doctrine in response is unavailing, and is indeed greeted with derision by the wolf:

> '3aa!' quod the volff. '3it pleyis thow agane?'   2671

The lamb is forced to try a new tack, that anyone has the right to a lawful trial, and he does so employing legal language somewhat desperately, stating that an accused should be able to:

> ... thairupon summond peremtourly
> For to propone, contrairie, or reply.   2685

The wolf, with an affectation of employing legal process, argues back:

> That is ane poynt and part of fals tressoun.   2695

The remorseless killing of the innocent lamb with a farcical pretence of legality is so stark as to arouse the narrator to sympathy, and to attempt to enlist the reader's support on the lamb's behalf also:

> Off his murther quhat sall we say, allace?
> Wes not this reuth, wes not this grit pietie,
> To gar this selie lamb but gilt thus de?   2704–6

Moralitas

A lengthy moralitas follows in which the lamb is compared to the poor and the wolf to their oppressors, of whom Henryson identifies three different kinds, each described in some detail, and then addressed individually. He begins with *fals peruerteris of the lawis* who pretend to do right but in reality accept bribes. These are exhorted to be conscious that God knows all and to *Hald with the richt*. The second are *mychtie men, haifand aneuch plentie*, who are nonetheless greedy and take as much as they can from the poor. Henryson addresses these men directly in an attempt to force them to see the error of their ways:

> O man but mercie, quhat is in thy thocht?
> War than ane wolf, and thow culd vnderstand!   2735–6

The third oppressor is the great landowner who exploits his tenants by leaving them too little to live upon; Henryson paints an affecting picture of the poor, forced:

> To leue vpon dry breid and watter caill.   2755

Much of the power of this moralitas comes from the direct nature of the address to the oppressors, in the form of apostrophe: *O man of law ... O man but mercie ... O thow grit lord*, and this is balanced by his threefold invocation of God in the final stanza, where he reverts to the metaphor of wolf and lamb.

13 The Paddock and the Mouse

The Taill of the Paddock & the Mous

The final tale is perhaps the bleakest of all.

Basic story: A mouse wishes to cross a river to where there is better food, but has no means of getting across till a paddock (a frog or toad) offers to take her over. The mouse is suspicious of the paddock's intention, seeing falsehood in his face, and requires the paddock to swear an oath to take her over safely; this he does, and has the mouse tie her leg to his. When they are in the water, the paddock tries to go under to drown the mouse, and the mouse tries to keep afloat. While this desperate struggle for life is going on, a kite is watching them. He flies over, grabs the pair by the thread which joins them, flies with them to the bank and kills them both, disembowels them and flays their skins off.

The *lytill mous* is immediately presented in human terms:

> Scho culd not swym; scho had na hors to ryde.   2780

One must ask whether the mouse's reasons for wanting to cross are intended to be seen as reprehensible: is the desire for better food a manifestation of that discontent with one's lot, which we have so often been enjoined to avoid? She does not say that she has no food on this side, only that it is not to her liking, and this should recall another mouse to mind.

In any case, the paddock's courteous offer has to be considered, but the mouse is somewhat put off by his appearance, which according to the pseudo-science of physiognomy, indicates *sumpart off falset and inuy*. The fundamental principle of *phisnomy* is outlined by the mouse in lines 2826–30, but is rejected by the paddock, who quotes scripture in his defence, causing *the hungrie mous* (driven by physical desires instead of prudence?) to snap: *Let be thy preiching*. At this moment, when the mouse shows interest in a means of passage, the paddock drops the courteous *ȝow / ȝe* which he has used hitherto and both speak to each other with the informal *thow / thy.*

The dramatic (in the sense of drama: of characters interacting) nature of the conversation between the two is a very prominent feature of this part of the poem; the mouse's impatience is emphasized by having her break into the paddock's stanza (ll.2851–3, and again in line 2859). In addition, the paddock's *be not agast* in line 2858 clearly indicates what the mouse's horrified reaction must have been to the suggestion that they tie themselves together. Only the paddock's swearing an oath will reassure the mouse, though earlier oaths have been little guarantee of steadfastness, and indeed, the fox who also swears to Jupiter (l.2026) that he will be true to the wolf in *The Fox, the Wolf and the Cadger*, then loses no time in betraying him. The reader's suspicions are confirmed by the narrator's comment:

> The mous thocht na thing bot to fleit and swym;
> The paddok for to droun set her intent   2877–8

The violence of the struggle in the river is vividly expressed by the verbs, and particularly by the accumulation of past tense verbs depicting intense physical action: *bowtit, forsit, preissit, forcit, plungit, cryit.* This is the occasion of one of Henryson's greatest imaginative *coups de théâtre.* We are wholly involved with the fatal struggle between the paddock and the mouse, and then with one line the viewpoint is completely altered and we are transferred to the wider perspective of the gled (i.e. a kite, a bird of prey):

> Fechtand thusgait, the gled sat on ane twist.   2896

From this moment on, nothing more is presented from the point of view of the paddock or the mouse; the verbs now refer to what the gled is doing to them: *claucht, flew, lowsit, slew, bowellit, fled.* These last two stanzas provide a devastating picture of the futility of their conflict and the randomness of fate, further underlined by the narrator's distance from events: *quhen I hard outred,* and:

> Giff this be trew, speir ȝe at thame that saw.   2909

Moralitas

A particularly close relationship is set up at the beginning of the moralitas with the words *My brother / Brother,* when Henryson deals with the general idea of

> Ane fals intent vnder ane fair pretence   2918

and gives the obvious warning to shun bad company, reinforced by
the refrain and the rhyme of the first four stanzas. Thereafter the
precise analogies are very apt: the paddock is man's body, the
mouse the soul, the water the world and of course the gled is
death. This conveys an accurate impression of the intended
relationship between soul and body, the former dependent on the
latter in this life, but also subject to its frailties, neatly expressed
by the mouse being bound to and pulled down by the paddock. The
final warning is of the suddenness of death and the need to be
prepared. This is also, of course, the ending not just of this fable,
but of the entire series, and the last stanza of all effectively closes
the work by bidding farewell to the reader in amicable terms:
Adew, my freind, taking a passing sideswipe at the friars'
predilection for a *sample or similitude* in their sermons, and
finally invoking the protection of Christ:

> Grant vs till pas in till ane blissit hour.   2975

Some thoughts on the Fables

The Fables are so varied in tone and content that it is not always
easy to have a consistent view of their message; sometimes the
pious moralitas seems at odds with the gleeful anarchy of the tale;
sometimes the moralitas provides a satisfying interpretation, at
other times it seems a laboured afterthought; at times the tale
seems to be told simply for the purpose of its elucidation; at other
times the poet's interest seems to lie primarily in the sheer
liveliness and hilarity of the events. The difference in tone
between the Aesopian and the Reynardian fables has already
been referred to, as has the apparent symmetry of the order in
which the fables have come to us. A further intriguing feature is
what seems to be the steadily darkening moral world as the fables
progress. A brief glance at the outcome of each of the fables will
suffice to illustrate this point:

i	Cock & Jasp	No suffering
ii	Two Mice	A fright only
iii	Cock & Fox	Victim gets serious fright; perpetrator escapes
iv	Fox & Wolf	Perpetrator is punished by death
v	Trial of Fox	Perpetrator is punished by death
vi	Sheep and Dog	Victim ends cheated and naked
vii	Lion and Mouse	Central fable: careless lion is almost put to death

viii	Preaching of Swallow	Careless birds are butchered
ix	Fox, Wolf & Cadger	Accomplice in crime is brutally beaten
x	Fox, Wolf & Husbandman	Accomplice in crime is abandoned in well
xi	Wolf & Wether	Brave but foolhardy victim is killed; killer escapes
xii	Wolf and Lamb	Innocent victim is killed; killer escapes
xiii	Paddock and Mouse	Innocent & guilty alike are killed, without reference to their culpability

The world of the later fables is altogether a bleaker and more perilous place.

What might we then be expected to take from a reading of Henryson's Fables? In the first place, they form a highly sophisticated work of art. Far from being a mere retelling of old stories, they have been selected, ordered and painstakingly organised by Henryson into a cohesive whole which articulates many of the concerns of his age. The overall structure of the work, with the introductory Prologue and the explanatory moralitas which then accompanies each tale, demonstrates Henryson's conscious organisation of his original material, and his exploitation of it for his own purposes. The first four stanzas of the Prologue emphatically assert the moral purpose of art, an indication of the seriousness of Henryson's intentions, and it is worthy of note that in more than half of the moralitates (e.g., numbers ii, iii, v, vii, viii, ix, xi, xiii) as well as performing the basic function of providing a moral interpretation of the tale, he explicitly returns to this same point, that stories may be used to point a moral:

> Now worthie folk, suppose this be ane fabill,
> And ouerheillit wyth typis figurall,
> ʒit may ʒe find ane sentence richt agreabill
> Vnder thir fenʒeit termis textuall. F586–9

This insistence on the moral purpose of art is one of the most outstanding features of the Fables, both in its assertion and in its practical application by means of the moralitates. The Prologue also provides the justification for Henryson's choice of these animal stories by stating that human beings in some aspects of their behaviour approach the condition of the animals:

> How mony men in operatioun
> Ar like to beistis in conditioun.   F48–9

Hence the eternal struggle between our spiritual aspirations and our carnal desires is expressed in terms of our likeness to animals. Man's habit of giving way to *lust and appetyte* means:

> That he in brutal beist is transformate   F56

and so we have a collection of tales in which animals exemplify human characteristics, good and bad: the vanity of the cock wins him a warning, the prudence of the swallow brings salvation, the wether's presumptuousness leads to his death. It must be stressed, however, that this is no idealised or simplistic moral world, where good behaviour is rewarded with good and bad with bad: the sheep is shown no mercy, some scheming foxes are killed, others escape with impunity, the innocent lamb is brutally slaughtered, the paddock and the mouse both die without reference to whatever qualities they might possess. Henryson is concerned with depicting the fallen world as it is (the sheep points out:

> Seis thow not, lord, this warld ouerturnit is … ?   F1307)

while using this information to suggest how it might be improved, were we to abjure our baser desires.

This theme of our resemblance to animals has the function of providing a unifying moral context to what would otherwise be a disparate collection of tales and is further reinforced by the moralitas which accompanies each tale.

Further evidence of the sophistication of the Fables as a work of art is supplied by the various techniques by which Henryson has developed and deepened his materials. The simple originals are dramatised, greatly lengthened, given powerful characterisation, authorial comment and incisive dialogue. Apart from the main characters of the fables, one should also note the constellation of lesser characters, such as *Gib Hunter, our iolie cat*, the list of *kennettis* named by the *wedow*, the wonderfully thrawn *gray stude mair* who kicks the wolf, the *fraudfull volff* who judges the sheep, the cadger, the husbandman and the shepherd who owns the wether. The quantity and variety of forms of direct speech are striking, including the urgent dialogue between swallow and the other birds, the pointed tension between the two mice, the formal set-piece statements of Chantecleir's hens, the fox musing on how it would just be typical if he were to be killed, the outraged incredulity of the wolf when the wether has lost his covering, the meticulous pleading of the lamb, the devious brilliance of any fox outwitting any wolf. This is an important method by which Henryson has transformed his originals and made them into something new and far more powerful.

Henryson's shaping hand is also to be seen in innumerable incidental details which have the effect of enriching the basic situations: the town mouse who *prunȝit forth in pryde*, the wool sticking to the fox's teeth, Freir Volff Waitskaith *with beidis in hand*, Father-war throwing his father's body into *ane peitpoit*, the birds in winter *neir slane with snaw and sleit*, the nekhering, *pypand lyke ane pertrik ee*, the fox running *hand in hand* with the wolf, while desperately trying to think up a ruse, the cabok *Quhyte as ane neip and round als as ane seill*, the little mouse who *had na hors to ryde*.

One of the most effective controlling devices which Henryson uses is his narrator, who does far more than merely tell the tales; he points the moral, often in the first person:

> This volf I likkin to ane schiref stout   F1265

often by intruding a moral sentiment into the tale itself:

> For falset failȝeis ay at the latter end.   F568

He preaches to the reader:

> Thir twa sinnis, flatterie and vaneglore,
> Ar vennomous: gude folk, fle thame thairfoir!   F612–3

sets up an amicable relationship with the reader:

> Freindis, heir may ȝe find ...   F365

he plays the part of the passer-on of information:

> I can not tell how eftirwart scho fure,
> Bot I hard say scho passit to hir den   F357–8

and in a more startling departure from the customary role of the passive narrator, he takes a part himself in several of the fables: he overhears the sheep's lament, is visited by Aesop in a dream and witnesses the birds being slaughtered. Once again, Henryson is providing in the device of the narrator a unifying element which binds the varied materials together to form a whole.

If it is true then that Henryson has imposed sense and order on the heterogeneous mixture of stories he took as his originals, what meaning may now be taken from them? There are two main areas where Henryson's purpose seems relatively plain. His attitude to the society around him seems to have been much of its time; he wishes for stability and security, but this is to be achieved by as little change as possible. The four-times-repeated moral of *The Two Mice* is to be content with what one has, however little it may be: the sheep, representing the poor crying to God for justice, can only conclude:

> We pure pepill as now may do no moir
> Bot pray to the: sen that we ar opprest
> In to this eirth, grant vs in heuin gude rest   F1318–20

and the loyal and conscientious wether is rebuked fcr his presumptuousness:

> Heir may thow se that riches of array
> Will cause pure men presumpteous for to be.   F 2595–6

Henryson's clarity of vision is unable to deny the many ills in our fallen world, but his social conservatism will not permit any radical reordering of that society. His suggestions for change in this life are limited to exhortations of better conduct by individuals, notably in the moralitas of *The Wolf and the Lamb*, in which he addresses various categories of oppressors of the poor, enjoining them to undergo a change of heart, in the best Dickensian manner:

> O thow grit lord, that riches hes and rent,
> Be nocht ane wolf, thus to deuoir the pure!   F2763–4

Perhaps the key to what seems to us now an ineffectual approach to social injustice lies in the assumption that the miseries of an earthly existence were to be tolerated in the expectation of a better life thereafter. Poor people,

> Of quhome the lyfe is half ane purgatorie   F2709

must simply prepare themselves for life after death:

> Ceis of 3our sin; remord 3our conscience;
> Do wilfull penance here; and 3e sall wend,
> Efter 3our deith, to blis withouttin end.   F793–5

In the end, the central concern of the Fables is the central concern of Christianity itself: the salvation of the individual, a theme which permeates the entire work. As might be expected in any work of its time, Christian beliefs and iconography are to be found throughout the Fables, from the parodies of confession and baptism in *The Fox and the Wolf*, to references to the Devil (2444), the Trinity (1648), the cross (2973), innumerable references to and invocations of God and occasionally of Mary (1139), quotations from scripture, most notably in the mouth of the lamb pleading for his life, the explicit statement that the swallow;

> The halie preichour weill may signifie   F1924

and the regular exhortations to pray. Even allowing for the increasing darkness and pessimism of the Fables, the striving for salvation is constantly asserted. The unhappy fates of the wether and the lamb, which seem so shocking to us, are considered solely in their earthly context, which by definition is of less importance than the future life. In the final fable, after the clinical dispatch of both paddock and mouse, we are encouraged still to be prepared for death:

> My freind, thairfoir, mak the ane strang castell
> Of gud deidis, for deith will the assay ...   F2966–7

while the final three lines of the entire poem specifically invoke the concept of redemption and the prospect of eternal life:

> Now Christ for vs that deit on the rude,
> Of saull and lyfe as thow art Saluiour,
> Grant vs till pas in till ane blissit hour.   F2973–5

THE TESTAMENT OF CRESSEID

Henryson's account of the fate of the unhappy Cresseid is one of the most powerful and affecting poems which has ever been written in these islands, and one which merits a far higher degree of awareness in the public consciousness than has hitherto been the case.

Background

The poem is based on a supposed series of events which occurred in the course of the Trojan war, that semi-historical, semi-legendary conflict which stocked the minds of Europeans with images for more than two thousand years. Even today the concept of the Trojan horse is widely recognised as a symbol of deceit and subversion. The story of Troilus and his fickle lover, affording elements of love, war and treachery, has attracted various writers (including Shakespeare in *Troilus and Cressida*) but Henryson's poem is based quite explicitly on the lengthy and sophisticated version of the story by Geoffrey Chaucer, his great English predecessor. Chaucer's *Troilus and Criseyde* is a powerful and influential work, dealing in five books with the love affair between the hesitant Troilus and the experienced Criseyde, and its unhappy ending. Henryson has consciously written a sequel to Chaucer's poem, in which he concentrates on the fate of the discarded Cresseid, and follows her to her death. It is highly ironic that the *Testament of Cresseid* was the best remembered of Henryson's works before the eighteenth century because it was often appended to editions of Chaucer's poem, and therefore was thought to have been written by Chaucer.

Henryson's narrative begins by assuming some knowledge of Chaucer's story and the characters involved, to which the following brief summary should be a useful introduction:

Chaucer's Troilus and Criseyde

(Priam and Hecuba are king and queen of Troy, and among their children are Hector, Troilus, Diophebe and Cassandra.)

Calchas flees from Troy to the Greek camp, leaving behind his daughter Criseyde, a widow, who is ashamed of her father's treachery, but continues to live privately in Troy. The warrior Troilus, who has never been ensnared by a woman, falls for Criseyde, but is unable to express his feelings for her. Pandarus, Criseyde's uncle, offers them the use of his house for clandestine meetings, and tricks Criseyde into staying with Troilus one night, which soon becomes a regular occurrence.

Meanwhile a truce is arranged for the purpose of swapping prisoners, and Calchas, wishing for his daughter to join him, asks the Greeks to swap one of their Trojan prisoners for Criseyde. When this is agreed the lovers are desolate, but Criseyde swears that she will be away no longer than ten days, and so departs. Diomede the Greek escorts her out of Troy and speaks to her in a friendly manner. She is reunited with her father and settles down. Troilus is inconsolable in spite of various diversions arranged by Pandarus, but when the tenth day comes, Calchas will not let Criseyde go back to Troy. Diomede begins to woo her, and after some time she gives him a brooch which Troilus had given her and accepts him as her lover. Troilus dreams that Criseyde has betrayed him, and Cassandra interprets the dream, adding that Criseyde is with Diomede. Troilus gradually and reluctantly begins to accept that she has left him. His brother Diophebe wins a coat from Diomede in the fighting and Troilus finds on it the brooch he had given Criseyde. He hopes to meet Diomede in battle, but is fated not to do so, and is himself killed by Achilles.

Basic story

Henryson begins his poem with a powerful picture of his elderly narrator protecting himself against the cold and diverting himself by reading Chaucer's *Troilus and Criseyde*, then taking another (unnamed) book in which he reads of Cresseid's unhappy end. After Diomede rejects her, she goes back to her father, keeping herself out of the public eye, and berates Venus and Cupid, blaming them for her unhappy situation. Thereupon she falls into a dream in which the seven planets appear before her, and at the request of Cupid they arraign Cresseid for her blasphemy. The verdict of the gods is that Cresseid is to be made ugly and to suffer pain and poverty, and specifically is to be stricken with leprosy. Cresseid awakes from the dream, but when she looks into a mirror she sees that she has indeed been stricken. Her father grieves with her, then accedes to her request to be conveyed in secret to the leper house outside the town. She makes a formal lamentation, regretting the loss of her former way of life, but is encouraged by another leper to begin to learn to make her living by begging, as lepers must, and this she does.

Meanwhile the victorious Troilus returns in triumph from battle and passes the place where Cresseid is sitting. The lepers ask him for alms and he listens to them. He looks at the deformed Cresseid without recognising her, but has the vague feeling that he has seen her before somewhere, since she reminds him of his former love. Accordingly he throws a purse of gold into her lap. The lepers are astonished by his liberality, but when Cresseid learns his name, she is inconsolable. Instead of blaming the gods, however, she now recognises that there is no-one to blame but herself. This being so, she sits down with a piece of paper and makes her testament, leaving her body to be consumed by the worms, all her possessions to be used to bury her, her ring given by Troilus to be returned to him, and her spirit to be left to the goddess Diana, to wander forever in waste woods. After her death a leper takes the ring to Troilus and tells him her story. Troilus grieves for her, but recognises that she was untrue. Finally, he erects a marble tomb over her grave.

The 616 lines of the poem may be made more accessible by being organised into sections as indicated below:

i   The introduction
ii   The beginning of the narrative
iii   Cresseid's dream
iv   Cresseid's leprosy
v   The Complaint of Cresseid
vi   The encounter between Cresseid and Troilus
vii   Cresseid's self-knowledge
viii The Conclusion

i   The Introduction (lines 1–70)

It was noted earlier that the Prologue to the Fables is to be seen as a very conscious statement by Henryson, in which he attempts to justify his enterprise and the manner in which he intends to execute it. This is no less true in the *Testament*, where, through the creation of the elderly narrator, Henryson raises again the question of the authenticity or orginality of a work of art and its relationship to its predecessors.

The first stanzas depict a bitterly cold evening, with the

narrator in his study trying to keep himself warm. It is essential to understand what has happened: the weather has been *richt feruent* (very hot) the sun is in Aries (March/April); the season is Lent (the six weeks before Easter) when unexpectedly cold weather has arrived from the north (*Fra Pole Artick*). This "blighted spring" takes on symbolic significance when Cresseid's fate is considered. It might be added that the astronomical situation outlined in the second stanza, the sun in opposition to Venus, cannot occur in nature, and should be taken as a forewarning of the extreme malevolence of the heavens. Also to be noted is the narrator's original purpose: to pray to Venus, the goddess of love, so that she would restore his *faidit hart*, but ironically, he finds it too cold and has to retreat to a room with a fire, where he laments the passing of the passions of youth. So we are given a picture of an elderly man who has loved in his youth, but who now needs the external comforts of a fire, a drink and a book; it is not surprising that he chooses a love story for consolation. In lines 41–2 he explicitly mentions that the book was written by *worthie Chaucer glorious*, and is in fact the story of Troilus and Cresseid. The praise he gives Chaucer is a fair reflection of the esteem in which the poet was held in the century after his death. Two stanzas (ll.43–56) recapitulate part of Chaucer's poem, dealing with the part where Cresseid has gone to the Greeks and Troilus awaits her return.

The next two stanzas repay close study: he says there is no need to repeat the details of Troilus's distress, since *worthie Chauceir* did it so well, but in line 61 he mentions *ane vther quair*, in which he read the story of Cresseid's end. We may safely assume that this other book was non-existent, and is a means of leading into his third reference to Chaucer by name, in the iconoclastic line:

Quha wait gif all that Chauceir wrait was trew?   64

In other words, Henryson is suggesting that however impressive Chaucer's version of the story may be, there may also be other versions which deal with aspects left unexplored by Chaucer, and it is one of these that he now intends to present to us. So just as the Fables were supposedly a version of Aesop, Henryson's original poem is supposedly validated by being a version, not of Chaucer, but of this unnamed *vther quair*.

ii   The beginning of the narrative (lines 71–140)

Henryson then begins his own narrative with a brief resume of
Cresseid's *desolait* position after her abandonment by Diomede,
but no sooner has he done this than he breaks in again in the
person of the narrator in two remarkable stanzas (ll.78–91) in
which he makes it clear that in spite of her admitted offences,
expressed in the words *filth ... fleschelie lust ... maculait ...
giglotlike ... foull plesance* his attitude is basically sympathetic to
her:

> I haue pietie thow suld fall sic mischance!   84

and:

> I sall excuse als far furth as I may.   87

This being so, it is really only with line 92 that the narrative
proper begins; although the narrator does appear again, it is
never with such a sense of his individual character, and indeed
the first person narrative, which has been used in every stanza so
far, saving those which merely retell Chaucer's story, is not used
again, other than in a conventional tag, till the very last stanza of
the whole poem.

   Henryson continues to evoke the reader's sympathy for
Cresseid by depicting the awkwardness of the life she feels
compelled to lead, out of the public eye: she has no friend, no
protector, moves about in disguise; when she speaks, she is
siching full soir; she is *with baill aneuch in breist* and *heuie in hir
intent*; she goes to the oratory to *weip hir wofull desteny*, but
perhaps unexpectedly she gives vent in her prayer to the feeling of
unfairness which the narrator has already mentioned. He
maintains that her fate was:

> nathing throw the gilt
> Of the ...   90–1

In her despair she attacks both Venus and her son Cupid, and in
an outburst which seals her fate, blames them for her situation:

> 'O fals Cupide, is nane to wyte bot thow
> And thy mother, of lufe the blind goddes!'   134–5

iii Cresseid's Dream (lines 141–343)

Henryson's presentation of the planets is one of his finest set-pieces, each celestial form being allocated two or three stanzas of description of traditional physical appearance and temperament. They appear in order, from the furthest to the nearest (according to the geocentric theory of the universe) and the characteristics which he attributes to them are to be found in many other mediaeval writings. **Saturn** is ill-tempered, with grey hair and clothing, and bearing all the signs of cold and age: *His teith chatterit*, and one of Henryson's deftest touches is the inclusion of the memorable detail:

> Out of his nois the meldrop fast can rin   158

... as also with his arrows, which are:

> Fedderit with ice and heidit with hailstanis.   167

In contrast to Saturn's greyness, **Jupiter**'s clothing is gold and green, and

> As goldin wyre sa glitterand was his hair   177

as befits the most joyful of the planets, who is:

> Fra his father Saturne far different.   171

The image of **Mars** as the god of war is still in the public consciousness today, and here he plays the part of:

> the god of ire,
> Of strife, debait, and all dissensioun   183–4

wearing various kinds of armour and bearing assorted weapons, *roustie* in colour, as befits the red planet,

> And at his mouth ane bullar stude of fome.   192

The sun, **Phebus**, receives his due as the giver of all life:

> And of the warld causing, be his mouing
> And influence, lyfe in all eirdlie thing   200–1

and the image is evoked of the king riding in his chariot, drawn by the four horses, here named Eoye, Ethios, Peros and Philogie.

The first point made about **Venus** is that she is present to defend both her son and herself; thereafter the main idea, expressed in several ways, is of her inconstancy; her very dress is:

> The ane half grene, the vther half sabill blak.   221

Her face shows *greit variance*; she is suddenly *changit and alterait*; with one eye she laughs, with the other weeps, and Henryson attributes this changeability to the fact that she is the goddess of love, which:

> Is sum tyme sweit, sum tyme bitter and sour,
> Richt vnstabill and full of variance,
> Mingit with cairfull ioy and fals plesance,
> Now hait, now cauld, now blyith, now full of wo,
> Now grene as leif, now widderit and ago.   234–238

The recorder of the proceedings is **Mercury**, *with buik in hand*, manifesting not only eloquence and ability with language, but also playing the part of a doctor of medicine.

The last of the planetary deities is **Cynthia**, the moon, who is often associated with changeability, being the heavenly body which more evidently alters to the naked eye, but here Henryson dwells more on the colour: *Of colour blak ... Haw as the leid, of colour nathing cleir ... Hir gyte was gray ...*

Mercury is chosen to be the *foirspeikar*, and commences by asking Cupide the purpose of the assembly. Cupide reports the insult given by Cresseid to himself and his mother, and Mercury advises that the highest and the lowest of the planets, Saturn and the Moon, should arbitrate in the matter and resolve the fate of Cresseid.

The pronouncement of the dreadful sentence on Cresseid is one of the most chilling passages in literature, and these stanzas repay careful study. The first indication of the nature of the sentence is the report that Cresseid will suffer:

> In all hir lyfe with pane to be opprest,
> And torment sair with seiknes incurabill,
> And to all louers be abhominabill.   306–8

But the effect is greatly deepened by the specifically physical action when Saturn lays *a frostie wand* on the sleeping Cresseid, and by the accumulation of alterations: from mirth to melancholy, from *moisture and heit* to *cald and dry*, from happiness to *greit diseis*, from riches to need. At this point, Henryson introduces another powerful device, an interruption of the narrative by the narrator himself in which he protests against the sentence, defends Cresseid and orders Saturn to withdraw the sentence. Much of the force of this stanza comes from the variety of forms of language he employs: the exclamation and address: *O cruell Saturne*; the denunciation of the sentence: *Hard is thy dome*; the question: *quhy hes thow na mercie ... ?*; the imperative: *Withdraw thy sentence*; and the final description of the sentence as *wraikfull* (= vindictive). But at the same time he recognises that such a withdrawal would require Saturn to be gracious, which he never was. Cynthia then reads her part of the pronouncement, made more effective by the structural parallelism in the listing of the specific and concrete examples of the changes Cresseid is to undergo:

> Thy cristall ene mingit with blude I mak,
> Thy voice sa cleir vnplesand hoir and hace,
> Thy lustie lyre ouirspred with spottis blak,
> And lumpis haw appeirand in thy face   337–340

and the final line of the Moon's statement makes explicit what till now has been only implied: as a punishment for her blasphemy against Venus and Cupid, Cresseid is to be stricken with leprosy. The people of the Middle Ages had a somewhat ambiguous attitude to this loathsome disease, which was still not uncommon in Scotland at the time. In the first place, the word was used loosely of various forms of skin trouble, though Henryson seems to have chosen a standard form of the disease to inflict on Cresseid, with dark lumps on the face, a hoarse voice, loss of hair and discoloration of the skin. The source of the disease was also a matter of some uncertainty. The belief that leprosy was a sexually transmitted disease had a long history, and is obviously relevant to Cresseid's situation. A disease might also be occasioned by astrological factors, such as the ominous conjunction of Saturn and the Moon in this poem. Finally, leprosy was often seen as a direct punishment from God for moral failings, Cresseid's blasphemy being an appropriate offence. The Bible affords various examples of such a punishment, while the obsessively detailed regulations for the isolation and ritualistic cleansing of lepers (e.g. in Leviticus xiii & xiv) further accentuate the fearful awe in which leprosy was held. While acknowledging the horror of the affliction, many people also regarded lepers as in some way specially marked by God, and under His protection. A leper was sometimes thought to be acting out his purgatory on earth, and hence to have attained a distinctive relationship with God. The mediaeval confusion between the beggar Lazarus, covered in sores, and the Lazarus whom Christ raised from the dead, as well as his healing of actual lepers, forged a connection between lepers and Christ and associated them with a path to eternal life not open to ordinary sinners. The widespread belief that King Robert I, the hallowed victor of Bannockburn, had latterly been a victim of the scourge helped to encourage this belief.

iv Cresseid's leprosy (lines 344–406)

The horror of Cresseid's sentence in the dream is made reality when she awakes, looks in a mirror, and sees that she has indeed become a leper. Given the reader's natural revulsion in these circumstances, it is significant to see how carefully Henryson continues to guide reactions in the direction of compassion for Cresseid, as he does here with the line:

> Gif scho in hart was wa aneuch, God wait!   350

There is great dramatic audacity in the introduction of the little servant *chyld* at this moment who knocks at the door to tell Cresseid that her father awaits her at dinner and that he says she has been praying long enough, adding the timely dramatic irony that:

> The goddis wait all ʒour intent full weill.   364

The relationship between father and daughter is delicately traced, with Cresseid's reference to *my father deir* (l.365) and his earlier greeting when she had been rejected by Diomede:

> Welcum to me; thow art full deir ane gest!   105

and so Calchas's shock is made almost palpable in his very physical reaction:

> He luikit on hir vglye lipper face,
> The quhylk befor was quhite as lillie flour;
> Wringand his handis, oftymes said allace
> That he had leuit to se that wofull hour.   372–5

The picture of father and daughter grieving together is an affecting one, whatever their culpability might have been, and once again Henryson guides the reader's reactions towards compassion with:

> Thus was thair cair aneuch betuix thame twane.   378

The shame they felt is clearly communicated by the phrases *in secreit wyse ... wonder priuely ... ane secreit ʒet ... that na man suld espy* which accompany her clandestine removal to the *spittaill hous*. Again Henryson directs the reader with:

> God wait gif Cresseid was ane sorrowfull gest   402

... when Cresseid lies alone in a corner of the leper house.

v The Complaint of Cresseid (lines 407–483)

For Cresseid's formal lamentation Henryson abandons the Rhyme Royal stanza which he has used throughout, as he does for Orpheus's lamentation in *Orpheus and Eurydice*, and adopts instead seven nine-line stanzas to bear the catalogue of pleasures which Cresseid must now lose, and the traditional contrast between the delights of the past and the suffering of the present. Cresseid does not accept nor allot responsibility for her plight, other than to the inscrutable workings of fate:

> Fell is thy fortoun, wickit is thy weird.   412

The elaborately formal address to herself in the second person in the first three stanzas is effectively dislocated by her breaking into her own voice:

> Vnder the eirth, God gif I grauin wer   414

before she lists the bedroom, the plate, the garments, the garden and so forth, which she now has lost. When she turns from the material possessions to her own person, she also turns from the distant second person to the intimate first, and her plaint is further underlined by Henryson's alliteration:

> My cleir voice and courtlie carrolling,
> Quhair I was wont with ladyis for to sing,
> Is rawk as ruik, full hiddeous, hoir and hace ...   443–5

When she turns to address the *ladyis fair of Troy and Grece*, she offers herself as an example of what might happen to them, but still regards herself merely as a plaything of fate, of *friuoll fortoun*, and indeed she ends with such a comment:

> Fortoun is fikkill quhen scho beginnis and steiris   469

– from which we may see that there is a touch of (however understandable) self-pity rather than self-knowledge in her words. The futility of this reaction is explicitly stated:

> Thus chydand with hir drerie destenye,
> Weiping scho woik the nicht fra end to end;
> Bot all in vane; hir dule, hir cairfull cry,
> Micht not remeid, nor ʒit hir murning mend.   470–3

and there is nothing for it but learning to beg like the rest of the
lepers.

vi The encounter between Cresseid and Troilus (lines 484–539)

This section brings with it one of the great moments, not only in
Henryson, but in European literature, when the triumphant
Troilus rides back to Troy with his spoils and passes the spot
where Cresseid and the other lepers are begging for alms. The
remarkable stanza depicting the meeting of the erstwhile lovers
without their knowledge is worth quoting in its entirety:

> Than vpon him scho kest vp baith hir ene,
> And with ane blenk it come into his thocht
> That he sumtime hir face befoir had sene,
> Bot scho was in sic plye he knew hir nocht;
> ʒit than hir luik into his mynd it brocht
> The sweit visage and amorous blenking
> Of fair Cresseid, sumtyme his awin darling.   498–504

This, the highest point of dramatic tension in the entire poem, is
distinguished by a remarkable proportion of monosyllables, a fine
example of the device of describing the deepest emotion in the
simplest language. Ironically the thought of Cresseid comes into
Troilus's mind, although he is unaware that it is the actual
Cresseid who has sparked it off. (Nor does Cresseid recognise
Troilus, as is clear from the line:

> And neuertheless not ane ane vther knew.   518

… and from her subsequent question on lines 533–4.) Troilus's
feeling for the Cresseid he had known is evident in his emotional
reaction to the thought of her; whether his throwing a purse of
gold into the lap of the fickle lover is intended to have significance
is at least debatable. When Cresseid is informed that their
benefactor was Troilus, *gentill and fre*, her remorse knows no
bounds.

vii Cresseid's self-knowledge (lines 540–574)

Cresseid gives vent to another lamentation, but one which has
none of the petulance of her earlier self, and which demonstrates
a proper appreciation of her moral state, necessary to whatever
form of salvation might be open to her. The repeated refrain
contrasting *fals Cresseid* with *trew knicht Troilus* is evidence
enough, though she enlarges on this by enumerating Troilus's
virtues and accusing herself of *fleschelie foull affection* and *lustis
lecherous*, and now acknowledges the fact of her own inconstancy:

> Becaus I knaw the greit vnstabilnes,
> Brukkill as glas, into my self ...   568–570

No mention now is made of Venus or Cupid, and she ends with a
clear recognition of her own culpability:

> Nane but myself as now I will accuse.   574

viii   The Conclusion

Having come to a full acceptance of her own moral failings,
Cresseid now makes her will, the testament of the title, leaving
her body to the *wormis and taidis*, her possessions to the lepers to
pay for her burial, and her ruby ring to be returned to Troilus. It
is intriguing to observe that after what seems to be her intended
conclusion, that is, *after* she says:

> Thus I conclude schortlie and mak ane end   586

and leaves her spirit to wander with Diana, the goddess of
chastity, she seems to have a moment of final regret and
frustration, remembering that the belt and brooch which Troilus
had given her are now in the possession of Diomede, and cannot
therefore be returned – *and with that word scho swelt*. It would
appear that, however much she may have come to some form of
self-knowledge, Henryson seems to have designed to have her die,
not at ease with herself, but still in some considerable
perturbance of mind. Whether her death is to be interpreted as a
specifically Christian resolution to the poem remains a matter of
conjecture; the pagan trappings of Diana and her *woddis and
wellis* do not of course exclude the themes of self-knowledge,
repentance and redemption.

One of the most notable features of the last few stanzas is the apparently brisk, or even brusque, manner in which Henryson tidies up after Cresseid's death: the leper man *sone* takes the ring, buries her *withouttin tarying*, goes *furthwith* to Troilus to inform him of her demise. Although Troilus exhibits the signs of emotional distress when he hears of her fate, his conclusion is unambiguous:

> Siching full sadlie, said, 'I can no moir;
> Scho was vntrew and wo is me thairfoir.'   601–2

Henryson continues to distance himself and the reader from the events by the deliberately vague *Sum said* in line 603 which qualifies all the information in the penultimate stanza, and carries as much, or as little, authority as the *sum men sayis* in line 77 which had hinted at Cresseid's promiscuity. The supposed inscription on Cresseid's grave is designed as a warning to *fair ladyis*, and the narrator, stepping forward in the last stanza, makes it explicit that *this ballet schort* has been written for their instructioun. The ending is as dismissively conclusive as we might expect:

> Sen scho is deid I speik of hir no moir.   615–6

This great poem stands as a powerful illustration of Henryson's virtuosity in combining classical and mediaeval or pagan and Christian features while skilfully using the writings of a great predecessor as a starting point for an original work. The most arresting element in the poem, Cresseid's leprosy, is Henryson's invention, while his questioning of Chaucer's version of events indicates a writer so confident in his own abilities as to set his interpretation beside Chaucer's, as if to challenge comparison.

ORPHEUS AND EURYDICE

The story of Orpheus and his lost wife Eurydice was one of the most popular tales throughout the Middle Ages, and appears in many versions, with many variations, some even with a happy ending. Henryson's poem is based both on the version by Boethius (c.480–524) and on the mediaeval commentary made by Nicholas Trivet, to both of whom he refers by name.

Basic story
Orpheus, son of Phoebus and Calliope, marries Eurydice, the queen of Thrace, and they live in bliss till the day when, fleeing from the advances of Aristaeus, she is bitten by a serpent and dies. Orpheus is desolate and laments her loss, then passes to the heavens to seek her, but without success. Eventually he arrives at the gate of hell, where he sees many horrors and many people who have died, and finally he meets Eurydice, in the company of Pluto and Proserpine. Orpheus plays his harp before them, and is given permission to take Eurydice away, on condition that he does not look back at her as she follows him. He accepts the condition, and they are almost at the outer gate of hell when he glances backward, and Eurydice is taken to the underworld forever.

The poem may be dealt with for convenience in several sections:

   i   Introduction and genealogy of Orpheus
   ii The narrative: the death of Eurydice
  iii The lament of Orpheus
  iv Orpheus's journey to the heavens
   v Orpheus's journey to hell
  vi The final loss of Eurydice
 vii The moralitas

i Introduction and genealogy of Orpheus (lines 1–91)

The poem begins in grand style with four stanzas in which Henryson asserts the importance of knowing the ancestry and lineage of a prince or lord, since one should follow the ways of one's ancestors:

> It is contrair the lawis of nature
> A gentill man to be degenerate.   8–9

In the third stanza he moves from the general statement of the
theme into the classical world, and assuming the persona of the
narrator:

> I say this be the grete lordis of Grewe   (*Greece*)   15

he indicates that he intends to speak of one of these, but that
following his own injunction, he will deal with his ancestry to
begin with.

Stanzas 5–9 (ll.29–63) deal with the Muses, the Nine sisters of
classical mythology, originally goddesses of various kinds of song,
and later thought to preside over one of the areas of the arts or
sciences. Their names are commonly given as Euterpe,
Melpomene, Terpsichore, Calliope, Clio, Erato, Polyhymnia,
Thalia and Urania. More recently, the idea of the Muse has been
taken generally to refer to the creative inspiration of an artist,
usually a poet. (The narrator of *Tam o' Shanter* relates how he is
unequal to the task of describing Nannie's dancing:

> But here my Muse her wing maun cour)

One of these Muses, Calliope, *of all musik maistresse*, is the
mother of Orpheus, by Phoebus (ll.61–2). Henryson then deals
with his growth to manhood, when the message from Eurydice,

> Requyrand him to wed hir and be kyng   77

indicates the appropriateness of the match between Orpheus and
the mychti quene of Trace, whose forwardness is again emphasised
in that:

> Hir erand to propone scho thocht no schame   80

In the last stanza of the introduction Henryson's picture of their
wedded bliss ends with the warning that worldly joy is like a
flower,

> Quhilk fadis sone, and endis with murnyng   91

– an ominous glimpse of what is soon to come.

ii The narrative: the death of Eurydice (lines 92–134)

The narrative proper begins at line 92, with the traditional, but in
this case misleading, opening of a pleasant May morning. This
joyful setting is a timely illustration of the transience of human
pleasure of which Henryson has just warned, and is immediately

to be rudely disturbed by the attempted rape of Eurydice by Aristaeus, *A bustuos herd*, who is overcome by the sight of her:

> Barfute, with schankis quhytar than the snawe.   99–100

In her desperate hurry to escape his advances, Eurydice stands on a poisonous snake and is bitten, whereupon Proserpine, queen of the underworld, calls her to her court. Perhaps there is evidence of another tradition in the phrases used by the handmaiden to inform Orpheus; she is *with the fary tane*;

> the quene of fary
> Claucht her wp sone and furth with hir can cary.   125–6

In his grief, Orpheus is now shown with his harp, preparing to make his lament.

iii   The lament of Orpheus (lines 134–183)

Orpheus's lament is marked off from the rest of the poem by a change in the stanza, as was the case with *The Complaint of Cresseid*. This takes the form of a ten-line stanza, with the affecting refrain:

> Quhar art thou gane, my luf Erudices?   143,153, 163

which is delicately modified, once by Orpheus himself, referring to

> My lady quene and luf, Erudices!   173

and once by the narrator, who refers to Orpheus who:

> Sore wepit for his wyf Erudices.   183

This carefully contrived lament has the effect of throwing the full weight of each stanza on the repeated last line, and in particular on the last word, in every case *Erudices*. The extensive use of alliteration further marks the lament as a formally organised piece. He addresses his harp, requiring it to share in his woe, and even though the birds of the wood sing and the very trees dance at his playing, he himself can receive no comfort. He bids farewell to his past life and his comforts, and asks his father Phoebus to lend his light as he determines to begin the search for his wife, under the direction of his grandfather, Jupiter:

> Throu thy god-hede, gyde me quhare scho is gone.   180

iv Orpheus's journey to the heavens (lines 184–246)

Henryson manages to convey Orpheus into the heavens with great ease and matter-of-factness, by referring the matter to his supposed source:

> Syne passit to the hevin, as sais the fable.   186

He begins his journey *By Wadlyng strete* (the Milky Way), in other words, at the outermost of the celestial spheres, that of the stars, and his travels thereafter are downwards and inwards, towards the earth at the centre of the system. His failure to find Eurydice is insistently stressed at each stage of the journey; even when Jupiter shows sympathy with his plight, the search of his sphere ends with the bald *Scho was noucht thare*, and it continues with *ȝit gat he noucht his wyf ... that lady come noucht thare ... Bot of his wyf thare knaulage gat he none ...* till he returns to the earth.

At this point Henryson includes some stanzas with details of the music which Orpheus learned in his passage, the music of the spheres themselves

> Causid be rollyng of the speris round.   222

The music of the spheres is referred to on a number of occasions by Henryson, as for example in *The Preaching of the Swallow*:

> And euerilk planet in his proper spheir,
> In mouing makand harmonie and sound   F1659–60

and is seen as a manifestation of the divinely-inspired harmony of the organisation of the universe. Orpheus's acquaintance with this music is a means of preparing him to play the role of the rational mind, which will be made explicit in the moralitas.

v Orpheus's journey to hell (lines 247–344)

The journeys to the heavens and to the underworld are separated not only by the three stanzas outlining Orpheus's musical learning, but also by a short intervention by the narrator protesting his own ignorance of music:

> For in my lyf I coud newir syng a note   242

which may be seen not only as the expected profession of modesty, but as a little joke on the part of an individual closely involved in musical education at the abbey school of Dunfermline.

Orpheus's lengthy journey, with its ballad-like overtones:

> Fer and full fer and ferther than I can tell   248

through what seems at times a very Scottish hell:

> Syne our a mure wyth thornis thik and scharp   289

eventually takes him to the gates of hell and the terrifying guardian Cerberus, the three-headed dog, who is the first denizen of the nether regions to be charmed by the playing of Orpheus's harp. In the same manner Orpheus lulls the Furies to sleep and releases three traditional sufferers from their torments by his playing: Ixion is enabled to leave the wheel on which he was bound, the water stays, allowing Tantalus to drink, and the vulture flees from its eternal feeding on Titius. In the depths of hell Henryson follows Virgil and Dante and many other writers in his lists of those to be found there: rulers like Nero or the Pharoah of the Book of Exodus,

> Quhilk in thair lyf rycht maisterfull had bene   319

and closer to his own time, the clergy who had betrayed their office:

> Thare fand he mony pape and cardinall,
> In haly kirk quhilk dois abusion.   338–9

vi The final loss of Eurydice (lines 344–414)

The *mychti quene of Trace*, once so lively and confident that she could summon Orpheus to wed her, is now:

> Lene and dedelike, pitouse and pale of hewe.   349

The atmosphere of dread in the halls of Pluto is deepened by Eurydice's guarded and fearful reply to Orpheus's asking how the change in her has come about:

> Quod scho, 'As now I dar noucht tell, perfay,
> Bot ye sall wit the cause ane othir day.'   357–8

The poem is structured to arouse expectations of hope when Orpheus begins to play to Pluto and Proserpine, since the skill of his music has overcome the infernal powers on several occasions before. As his *warison*, his minstrel's reward, he asks for permission to take Eurydice away, and this is granted, but with the fatal condition:

> Gyf thou turnis, or blenkis behind thy bak,
> We sall hir haue forewir till hell agayn.   382–3

Much of the fascination of this story lies in our appreciation of how close Orpheus comes to gaining his desire, and of the inevitability of his failure. Henryson recognises this very human tension in the matter-of-fact:

> Quhat will ye more? In schort conclusioun,
> He blent bak-ward and Pluto come anone,
> And vnto hell agayn with hir is gone.   391–3

vii The Moralitas (lines 415–633)

This moralitas of more than two hundred lines is on a different scale from those appended to the Fables, and in a different verse format, adopting rhyming couplets in place of the seven-line stanza. Although a few of the Fables have moralitates approaching (and occasionally surpassing, as in *The Cock and the Jasp, The Sheep and the Dog* and *The Wolf and the Lamb*) this proportion, the sheer length permits Henryson rather more leisurely development of the themes.

As so often in the Fables, Henryson begins by establishing a relationship between the narrator and his audience, with the first words: *Lo, worthy folk.* He goes on to acknowledge his sources in Boethius and Trivet, then adopts the analogical technique employed in the Fables by applying specific qualities to the characters in the tales, and he follows tradition in ascribing to Orpheus:

> ... the part intellectiue
> Of mannis saul and vnder-standing, free
> And separate fra sensualitee.   428–30

Hence Orpheus's identification with music, which is seen as a manifestation of harmony, organisation and rationality. The symbolism of music being used to control all kinds of dangers, known and unknown, fits ideally the notion of the rational part of the mind being used to control the irrational, and to prepare the soul to face all kinds of perils.

Eurydice on the other hand represents:

> oure affection,
> Be fantasy oft movit vp and doun   431–2

– that is to say, the emotional aspects of the human soul, sometimes tending towards spirituality, sometimes towards sensuality. The intrinsically misogynist post-classical civilisation found less difficulty with this concept that we might today.

The traditional equivalence between Aristaeus, the would-be rapist of Eurydice, and *gude vertewe*, however strange it may at first sight appear, is at least partly explained by the mediaeval belief that his name was derived from the Greek word for 'best', and so just as he is transformed from evil to good, the delightful meadow of the beginning of the narrative is transformed, as sometimes in the Fables, into a symbol of *this warldis wayn plesance*, into which Eurydice ran, to be attacked by the serpent of sin.

> Than parfyte reson wepis wondir sare,
> Seand oure appetite thusgate mys-fare.   445–6

Orpheus's journey to the heavens, then, is seen as a dramatisation of the human quest for *the lyf contemplatyve*, which must fail while we are so bound in our physical bodies.

After some thirty or forty lines of interpretation, some immediacy is imparted to the verse by the personal appeal to Orpheus to desist from his fruitless quest in the heavens:

> Sir Orpheus, thou seekis all in vayn
> Thy wyf so hie; thar-for cum doun agayn   459–60

and confront Cerberus, whose three heads threaten humans in each of the three stages of life. Here Henryson expounds for us the significance of Orpheus's soothing of Cerberus:

> Bot quhen our mind is myngit with sapience,
> And plais apon the harp of eloquence   469–70

then:

> This dog oure saule has no power to byte.   474

Retracing Orpheus's journey through hell, Henryson comes to the three sufferers, Ixion, Tantalus and Titius, with an account of the misdeeds which brought them to this pass. He then relates each of these three stories to the basic theme of the moralitas, whereby reason has the function of controlling affection, or irrationality. He explains the wheel on which Ixion was bound in terms of the familiar mediaeval concept of the wheel of fortune; just as Orpheus's playing had the effect of stilling the wheel, so when again we use our *reson and perfyte sapience*, then:

> ... the grete sollicitude,
> Quhile vp, quhile doun, to wyn this warldis gud,
> Cessis furthwith ...   515–7

Tantalus

> Betakenis men gredy and couatose   532

and so suffers the thirst of covetousness, but when *reson and intelligence* play on the *harp of eloquence*, he is enabled to drink as he wishes,

> Of couatise to slake the birnand thrist.   558

Titius has offended Apollo by dabbling in *the craft of diuinacion* and so suffers his gruesome punishment, but when Orpheus plays, *That is, our vndirstanding*, then:

> This perfyte wisdome with his melody
> Fleyis the spreit of fenӡeid profecy,
> And drawis vpwart our affectioun
> Fra wichcraft, spaying and sorsery.   585–8

The identification is made quite specific in the phrase *Than Orpheus, our ressoun* (l.610) and the moral point of the story summed up in:

> Than Orpheus has won Erudices,
> Quhen oure desire wyth reson makis pes   616–7

and Orpheus's backward look is therefore a backsliding to *warldy lust for the affection*. Again, the transmutation of the spirited and attractive queen of Thrace into an negative image of sensuality, ensnaring the virtuous man, is part of the outlook of the age.

This poem has suffered by comparison with the Fables and *The Testament of Cresseid*, since it has been regarded as a more uneven and over-bookish work. There are, of course, few works which would not be overshadowed when compared with these two, and it is really a simple matter to perceive the many great merits which it possesses, particularly in the narrative section and in the lament of Orpheus. Once more, this is a poem which deserves to be better known, even among students of Henryson.

ROBENE AND MAKYNE

This delightful little poem, partaking both of the ballad tradition
and of the French *pastourelle*, a poem of rustic courtship involving
a debate or discussion, was for long the best known of Henryson's
works, having been included in various anthologies in the
eighteenth century. The deftness of its handling, the wry accuracy
of its depiction of the behaviour of lovers and the sparse irony
with which it is recounted make it one of the most accomplished
works of its period, and as such, one which should be far more
widely known.

The simple situation of the reluctant Robene and the ardent
Makyne is worked out largely on a structure of antithetical
stanzas, the first six (and a later four) spoken alternately. In the
place of the third party who has the affections of one of the
estranged lovers, Robene has his responsibilities to his flock of
sheep, which he uses as an excuse for his less than satisfactory
response to Makyne's passionate outpourings. The first words of
the poem introduce Robene looking after his sheep, a leisurely
occupation contrasted with the vigour and directness of Makyne's
address:

> Robene sat on gud grene hill
> Kepand a flok of fe;
> Mirry Makyne said him till,
> 'Robene, thow rew on me!'   1–4

Protesting that he knows nothing of love, he claims that he is
concerned only with watching his sheep, pointing them out with
affected insouciance:

> Lo quhair thay raik on raw.   12

He plays the old male game of pretending not to be familiar with
the very terms which Makyne uses:

> Or quhat is lufe, or to be lude?
> Fane wald I leir that law.   15–16

Makyne's retort is painstaking in its literalness:

> At luvis lair gife thow will leir,
> Tak thair ane ABC: 17–18

Robene repeats that he knows nothing of love, but cannot
understand why she is so upset, given that:

> The weddir is fair and I am fane,
> My scheip gois haill aboif   29–30

and he adds the perhaps intentionally infuriating detail that if
they were to indulge in love making, his sheep would disapprove!

> And we wald play ws in this plane,
> Thay wald ws bayth reproif.   31–2

The intensity of Makyne's feeling is a painful counterpoint to
Robene's calculated indifference, particularly when she offers him
all she has:

> And thow sall haif my hairt all hail,
> Eik and my madenheid.   35–6

Robene, with all the casual cruelty of the loved who does not love
in return, takes full advantage of Makyne's eagerness, offering
her the possibility that he might be interested the following day,
but only if his sheep are not neglected! He ends with the less than
consoling suggestion that she should cheer up:

> Makyn, than mak gud cheir.   48

At this point Henryson greatly intensifies the dramatic action by
moving from the alternate stanzas of speech to alternating pairs
of lines, from which the characters and the differing standpoints
of the two are most skilfully revealed and counterpointed.
Makyne is near despair, Robene near simple rudeness:

> 'Robene, I stand in sic a styll;
> I sicht, and that full sair.'
> 'Makyne, I haif bene heir this quhyle;
> At hame God gif I wair.'
> 'My huny Robene, talk ane quhyll,
> Gif thow will do na mair.'
> 'Makyne, sum vthir man begyle,
> For hamewart I will fair.'   57–64

Two stanzas of narrative follow, retaining the opposition between
the two by continuing to allot them alternate pairs of lines as they
go off in different directions and greatly differing moods:

> Robene on his wayis went,
> Als licht as leif of tre;
> Mawkin mvrnit in hir intent,
> And trowd him nevir to se.   65–6

As we might expect, Makyne goes off to weep, while Robene busies himself by assembling his sheep, but in an ironic reversal of roles, Robene begins to experience something of the pangs of love, and pursues Makyne to convince her of his conversion. It is unfortunate that his love-plea is qualified by an assurance that:

> My scheip to morne quhill houris nyne
> Will neid of no keping. 87–8

It is fitting that he receives his answer in the form of a proverb:

> 'Robene, thow hes hard soung and say
> In gestis and storeis auld,
> "The man that will nocht quhen he may
> Sall haif nocht quhen he wald."' 89–92

His imploring invitation, asserting the mildness of the evening and the absence of intruders, is matched now by the measured calm of a woman who fully understands herself and him:

> 'Robene, that warld is all away,
> And quyt brocht till ane end ... ' 105–6

as she recognises what has been the nature of their relationship hithero:

> 'For of my pane thow maid it play,
> And all in vane I spend' 109–110

and neatly turns the tables on him by reminding him of his behaviour to her when he was in a position of power:

> 'As thow hes done, sa sall I say,
> "Mvrne on, I think to mend."' 111–112

His final plea, with its importunate declarations of undying love is conclusively rebuked by Makyne's:

> 'Robene, with the I will nocht deill;
> Adew, for thus we mett.' 119–120

The last stanza of narrative has the positions reversed, with Makyne *blyth annewche*, and Robene *In dolour and in cair*, while the final touch of grim ironic humour leaves Robene where he had wished to be:

> Kepand his hird vnder a huche,
> Amangis the holtis hair. 127–8

There can be few poems which so adequately illustrate the abilities of a major poet in such small compass as this one. Its terse, understated exposition of the range of emotions experienced by the lovers, its formal excellence, the delicate balance between passion and wry humour, and the economical characterisation all combine to produce a poem of remarkable quality and attractiveness.

THINGS TO THINK ABOUT

Among the many areas of interest to which these poems give rise, some particular consideration should be given to a few basic ideas, some to do with the manner of the writing and some with its content. Two of the most important stylistic devices in the poems are **the role of the narrator** and the use of **direct speech**, both of which have been mentioned in passing above, but which are fundamental to a proper understanding of the poems.

There are various easily identifiable techniques by which Henryson creates the narrator in his poems. A frequent device is his use of conversational, line-filling **tags**, which create the sense of a casual, chatty relationship with the reader:

> I wis (F27 & 1662 & 2960)
> as I haif tauld (F57)   I yow assure (F137)

In many places, but particularly in the moralitates, he uses a **personal address to the reader**:

> my maisteris (F29)
> Freindis (F365)   Lo, worthy folk (O&E415)
>
> My brother (F2910)   Now worthie wemen (T610)

An extension of this is the use of the **first person** generally, which keeps an eye on the progress of the narrative, and reminds us that an individual is telling it:

> Thairfor I ceis and will na forther say (F160)
> I say this be Erudices the quene (O&E92)
>
> I can not tell how eftirwart scho fure/
> Bot I hard say scho passit to hir den   (F357–8)

Another personalising factor is the **appeal to authority**, by which he tries to convince us that he has found information in some other source, and is merely passing it on, or commenting on it:

> Ane cais I fand quhilk fell this ather yeir   (F409)
>
> In Metaphisik Aristotell sayis   (F1636)

Perhaps the most powerful means of emphasising the narrator is in the use of **personal appearance**, where he is a character in the poem, which applies in *The Preiching of the Swallow* and the *Testament* (and also in parts of *The Lion and the Mouse* and in the moralitas of *The Sheep and the Dog*):

I mouit furth betuix midday and morne
Vnto the hedge vnder the hawthorne grene,
Quhair I befoir the said birdis had sene ...   (F1780–2)

And in my dreme, me thocht come throw the schaw
The fairest man that euer befoir I saw.   (F1347–8)

In the *Testament*, the creation of the narrator is inevitably on a much larger scale altogether. Henryson uses the introductory section (ll.T1–70) to impart to the reader a great deal of information about the narrator-persona, the time, season of the year, place, weather, his age and state of mind:

I mend the fyre and beikit me about,
Than tuik ane drink, my spreitis to comfort.   (T36–7)

We learn that he gets the idea from Chaucer (T40–2) and from *"ane vther quair"* (T61) and his independence of spirit is asserted when he questions Chaucer's version:

Quha wait gif all that Chauceir wrait was trew?   (T64)

When the narration begins, he reveals something of himself by his so clearly siding with Cresseid, by his scathing aside on Diomeid:

Quhen Diomeid had all his appetyte,
And mair, fulfillit of this fair ladie ...   (T71–2)

... and by his explicit comment:

I sall excuse als far furth as I may ...   (T87)

Thereafter, there is little first-person narrative intrusion, throughout the direct speech or the Complaint (though of course he continues to manipulate our reaction to events, not least in his remarkable outburst against Saturn's sentence, ll.323–329) till the narrator returns with a final admonition and the dismissive:

Sen scho is deid I speik of hir no moir.   (T616)

A first-person narrator also introduces *Orpheus and Eurydice*, but with none of the elaboration of character seen in the *Testament*, and shapes the moralitas with acknowledgments to his original sources, Boethius and Trivet:

I sall the tell sum part, as I haue red.   (O&E490)

It is undoubtedly part of the attractiveness of *Robene and Makyne* that, in the few lines of the poem which are not dialogue, the narrator is self-effacing to a remarkable degree, only occasionally underlining an emotion:

> Robene on his wayis went,
> Als licht as leif of tre   (R&M65–6)

or marking the turning-point of the poem:

> Be that, sum pairte of Mawkynis aill
> Outthrow his hairt cowd creip.   (R&M77–8)

The narrator is left to inform the reader of the final situation:

> Scho sang, he sichit sair   (R&M124)

and this spareness of narratorial intervention has the effect of intensely concentrating emotion on the direct interaction of the two characters.

Henryson's handling of **direct speech** throughout the poems is masterly and is one of the most important devices which he employs, almost half of all the lines in the Fables (excluding the moralitates) being in the form of direct speech. There are various forms which this takes, for example, the very frequent **vigorous interchange of opinion** between characters, as with the two mice, or the paddock and the mouse:

> 'Sister, is this ȝour dayly fude?'
> 'Quhy not,' quod scho, 'think ȝe this meit
>   nocht gude?"   (F209–210)
> 'I sall the leir to swym—be not agast—
> Als weill as I.' 'As thow?' than quod the mous.   (F2859–60)

This often involves short statements and counterstatements, the swift interchange of speaker, direct questioning (or insult) and the use of significant addresses which indicate the perceived respective status of the speakers, such as *thow / ȝe,* or *Schir / carll.*

In almost all of the Fables can be found a character who employs carefully **reasoned argument or pleading**, like the sheep or the lamb:

> Thocht I can nocht, nature will me defend,
> And off the deid perfyte experience:
> All heuie thing man off the sellf discend,
> Bot giff sum thing on force mak resistence;
> Than may the streme on na way mak ascence
> Nor ryn bakwart; I drank beneth ȝow far:
> Ergo, for me ȝour bruke wes neuer the war.   (F2644–2650)

... where the argument is carried by modifying words like *Thocht ... and ... bot ... than ... nor,* and finally *Ergo.* Some other features of this form of speech are the complex sentences with carefully logical development, the adducing of evidence and a tone of calm reason (sometimes spurious, as with the various foxes). Examples can be found when the mouse pleads with the lion (e.g. ll.1496–1502) or the fox persuades the wolf to try for the nekhering (ll.1035–2041). Although the swallow also uses these devices, it is interesting that the distinctive urgency of his speech is conveyed by a great variety of techniques, in particular the imperative verbs. The paddock's language changes notably from elaborate persuasion to more direct statement with imperatives as soon as the mouse snaps at him *Let be thy preiching* (l.2851)

A device often used to convey extremities of feeling is **formal, ritualised statement** from individuals talking sometimes to other characters, but more often to themselves or to characters not actually present, such as the cock's quest for truth when confronted with the jasp, the sheep's overheard complaint to God, Cresseid's Complaint, or her outspoken attack on Venus and Cupid. Standard features include exclamation and apostrophe:

> O gentill jasp, O riche and nobill thing   (F79)

> O fals Cresseid and trew knicht Troylus!   (T546)

... parallelism of structure, rhetorical question:

> Quhar suld thow mak thy habitatioun?   (F106)

> Wait thow nocht wele I am thi barne and child?   (O&E166)

and sometimes a refrain as in Cresseid's Complaint or Orpheus's lamentation:

> Quhar art thow gane, my luf Erudices?   (O&E143&c)

Finally, perhaps the most affecting of all the forms of direct speech occurs when Henryson eschews all elaboration and uses the simplest language possible. The touching intimacy of the relationship between Cresseid and her father comes from the sheer **simplicity and directness** of the (largely monosyllabic) dialogue and its surroundings:

> And sa he did, and said, 'Douchter, quhat cheir?'
> 'Allace!' quod scho, 'Father, my mirth is gone!'
> 'How sa?' quod he ...   (T367–9)

The same kind of directness can be found at other moments of heightened emotion, for instance, Orpheus hearing the news of Eurydice's death:

Till at the last schir Orpheus couth heir,
And of hir cry the caus than can he speir.
Scho said, 'Allace, Erudices 3our quene,
Is with the fary tane befor myne ene!'   (O&E116–9)

or Troilus's dismissal of Cresseid:

'I can no moir;
Scho was vntrew and wo is me thairfoir.'   (T601–2)

In addition to the stylistic elements in the poems, no study is complete without consideration of the thematic elements, two of the most vital being the **social and political content** and the **moral purpose** of the poems.

Henryson's Fables express a fairly consistent attitude to society, some of them dealing explicitly with social problems, in particular the misuse of power, as in *The Sheep and the Dog* and *The Wolf and the Lamb*. The writer recognises the many ills which people suffer, but counsels stoic forbearance; the sheep, even after invoking God, has no redress but the prospect of the afterlife; *after* the slaughter of the lamb, Henryson expresses the hope:

God keip the lamb, quhilk is the innocent,
From wolfis byit and men extortioneris   (F2770–1)

and much of the moralitas is taken up with the slightly desperate wish that wicked men will change their ways. One source of Henryson's sensitivity to the abuse of power would be his expertise in legal matters, which, apart from the likelihood that he studied law and practised as a notary public, is evident from many of the fables. Some fables have a setting which is entirely based on legal procedure, *The Trial of the Fox* and *The Sheep and the Dog* being the most obvious and providing examples of justice being employed and misemployed; the lamb also invokes the law, which is powerless to protect him. Elsewhere, legal vocabulary, imagery and other references abound: Chantecleir's hens

Fell of that cace in disputatioun;   (F494)

the husbandman demands that the wolf produce a witness; the mouse reminds the lion that *mercy and reuth* (l.1468) should be the attributes of a judge; the *man of law* is enjoined to *let be thy subteltie* (l.2721), and even Aesop himself claims that he:

In ciuile law studyit full mony ane day.   (F1373)

Other fables may deal less exclusively with social matters, but the underlying (and indeed often the explicit) message is the pressing

need to maintain the structure of society, however imperfect: the
moralitates of both *The Two Mice* and *The Wolf and the Wether*
stress in different ways the dire consequences of moving out of
one's station in life. Perhaps the most significant instance of
Henryson's concern for stability is to be found in the central fable
of *The Lion and the Mouse*, where the roles and the
responsibilities of the common people, the nobility and the king
himself are expounded. A neglectful king invites turbulent nobles
to oppress the poor, and so the central element in the social
system is a conscientious ruler who restrains those of ill intent:

> And God, as thow all rychteous prayer heiris,
> Mot saif our king, and gif him hart and hand
> All sic wolfis to banes of the land.   (F2774–6)

Finally, it is no exaggeration to assert that Henryson's main
concern in all his work, often explicitly stated, would be for the
poems to have a readily ascertainable moral function. This idea,
that the purpose of the poems is not just to entertain, but to
convey a moral message, is reinforced by being expressed in a
number of ways. One of the most obvious of these is Henryson's
frequent **explicit comments** on the topic, often in figurative
language, for example in the Prologue:

> Sa lyis thair ane doctrine wyse aneuch
> And full of frute, vnder ane feinȝeit fabill ...   (F17–18)

The moral purpose is made similarly unmistakable by the use of
the **Moralitates**, with their frequent explanations or inter-
pretations of the story which has just been told:

> This feinȝeit foxe may weill be figurate
> To flatteraris with plesand wordis quhyte ...   (F600–1)

> This vgly way, this myrk and dully streit,
> Is nocht ellis bot blinding of the spreit   (O&E600–1)

and their admonitions or exhortations to follow a particular line of
advice:

> Thir twa sinnis, flatterie and vaneglore,
> Ar vennomous: gude folk, fle thame thairfoir!   (F612–3)

> Pray we thairfoir quhill we ar in this lyfe ...   (F1944)

At frequent intervals throughout the poems, Henryson includes
proverbial phrases, or expressions of wisdom:

For wyfis sayis that lukand werk is licht.   (F102)

3it efter ioy oftymes cummis cair,
And troubill efter grit prosperitie.   (F290–1)

sometimes expressed in the form of similes:
As fitchis myngit ar with nobill seid,
Swa intermellit is aduersitie
With eirdlie ioy ...   (F367–9)

and these traditional-sounding saws relate the happenings of the tales to a wider background and so further help to provide a moral context for their interpretation.

Finally, the moral purpose is expressed **in the action**, whereby the evil are (sometimes) punished and the good (sometimes) prosper. Think of the respective punishments allotted to Troilus and to Cresseid; how just are these? The little birds were lazy and improvident; do they deserve their fate? What about Orpheus? Or the Paddock and the Mouse? Do they deserve theirs? What is meant by *deserving*, anyway? Think also of the point of view taken by Henryson (or by the narrator), especially in the *Testament*, where he so clearly sides with Cresseid, and contrast this with her own (and Troilus's) sense of what she *deserves*.

It is fitting to end with the idea of moral purpose, since the most important purpose of Henryson's artistic life, from his own point of view, would have been to assist individuals in their never-ending struggle towards personal salvation. In a secular age, it may be difficult for us to see that, despite their often pagan settings, the three major poems return again and again to this central concept of Christianity. The interpretation of Orpheus as our reason overcoming the attractions of Eurydice, our affection, is another embodiment of the eternal battle to gain eternal life. Whether the wretched Cresseid's ultimate growth towards a form of self-knowledge means that she has also attained salvation seems to be left deliberately unclear, while the primary emphasis of the Fables is on the need to make prudent and informed choices in life, so that we may avoid all distractions from the main business of this life: preparation for the next. It is well to remember that in the first of the fables, Henryson declares that:

This gentill iasp, richt different of hew,
Betakinnis perfite prudence and cunning   (F127–8)

and there is at least a sense in which this idea is indeed the key to
a proper understanding of the poems, as Henryson himself
implies. *Prudence and cunning* (that is, knowledge) are virtues
available to anyone, though they are often disregarded:

> Bot now, allace, this iasp is tynt and hid.
> We seik it nocht, nor preis it for to find   (F155–6)

but ultimately the message is of our individual responsibility for
the conduct of our own lives:

> Ga seik the iasp, quha will, for thair it lay.   (F161)

RECOMMENDED READING

(a) The Scots Language

For those wishing a brief introduction to the topic, an excellent short (eight pages) account of the history and present state of the language can be found in: *The Concise Scots Dictionary* ed. Mairi Robertson (Aberdeen University Press 1985)

More developed accounts are:

ed. A.J. Aitken: *Lowland Scots* Edinburgh 1978 (ASLS Occasional Paper No. 2)
eds. A.J. Aitken & Tom McArthur: *Languages of Scotland* Chambers 1979 (ASLS Occasional Paper No.4)
Billy Kay: *Scots: The Mither Tongue* (Mainstream 1986/Grafton 1988)
J. Derrick McClure: *Why Scots Matters* Edinburgh (Saltire Pamphlet 1988)
David Murison: *The Guid Scots Tongue* Edinburgh (Mercat Press 1984)

Two essays dealing more particularly with the literary language are:

Alex Agutter: *Middle Scots as a Literary Language* in: The History of Scottish Literature Vol.1 ed. R.D.S. Jack (Aberdeen University Press 1988)
A.J. Aitken: *The Language of Older Scots Poetry* in: ed. J. Derrick McClure: Scotland and the Lowland Tongue (Aberdeen University Press 1983)

(b) Editions of Henryson

The most complete recent edition of the poems is *The Poems of Robert Henryson* ed. Denton Fox (Oxford 1981); the full text is also available in paperback with brief notes.

Other editions include those edited by H. Harvey Wood (Edinburgh Mercat Press 1933/58) and Charles Elliott (Clarendon 1963/74).

Some selections available include:

Selections from the Poems of Robert Henryson ed. David Murison
    (Edinburgh 1951)
Selected Poems of Robert Henryson ed. W.R.J. Barron (Manchester
    Carcanet 1981)
Selected Poems of Henryson and Dunbar eds. Bawcutt & Riddy
    (Edinburgh Scottish Academic Press 1992)

An interesting volume still sometimes to be found is Hugh
Macdiarmid's choice of Henryson's poems with an introductory
essay in Penguin's *Poet to Poet* series.
ed. Hugh Macdiarmid: *Robert Henryson* (Penguin 1973)

Editions of *The Testament*:

The Testament of Cresseid ed. Bruce Dickins (London Faber
    1925/43)
The Testament of Cresseid ed. Denton Fox (London 1968)

One edition of the Fables which may be found useful is that edited
by George D. Gopen: *Morall Fabillis of Esope the Phrygian*
(Indiana & Edinburgh 1987) which has an English translation
accompanying the text.

(c) Commentary and Background

After centuries of neglect a proper critical discourse has begun to
emerge in recent years. This first short piece is included as being
probably the most readily available:

Patrick Cruttwell: *Two Scots Poets: Dunbar and Henryson* in: The
Age of Chaucer ed. Boris Ford. Pelican Guide to English
Literature Vol. 1. Penguin 1954 (pp.175-87)

A more recent short essay is:

John MacQueen: *Poetry James I to Henryson* in: The History of
    Scottish Literature Vol. 1 ed. R.D.S. Jack (Aberdeen University
    Press 1988)

Fuller studies:

Douglas Gray: *Robert Henryson* (Leiden 1979)
Robert L. Kindrick: *Robert Henryson* (Boston 1979)
Matthew P. McDiarmid *Robert Henryson* (Edinburgh 1982)
John MacQueen: *Robert Henryson: A Study of the Major Poems* (Oxford 1967)
Marshall W. Stearns: *Robert Henryson* (New York 1949)

(d) Cassettes

Recordings of some of the poems are available from Scotsoun, 13 Ashton Road, Glasgow G12 8SP:

Scotsoun Makars Series: two cassettes containing six fables, the *Testament, Orpheus and Eurydice, Robene and Makyne* and the *Garmont of Gud Ladeis*, with an introduction by Matthew McDiarmid.
Robert Henryson – The Makar: Some thoughts and reflections by R.J. Lyall.

Other cassettes, including a performance text of *The Preiching of the Swallows* are available from the **Robert Henryson Society** which was founded in Dunfermline in 1993 and which serves as a focus for the study of Henryson, collecting materials, publishing a newsletter and offering a number of events each year, including an annual day of Henryson-related activities. The society may be contacted by writing to:

> The Hon. Secretary
> The Robert Henryson Society
> c/o Abbey Park House
> Dunfermline KY12 7PB